HERSHEY'S
TIME·LESS
DESSERTS

ideals®

Ideals Publishing Corp.
Nashville, Tennessee

CONTENTS

Director of Publishing: Patricia Pingry
Managing Editor: Marybeth Owens
Cookbook Editor: Shelly Bowerman
Copy Editor: Cornell M. Brellenthin
Art Director: Patrick McRae
Photographer: Gerald Koser
Food Stylist: Lisa Landers
Editorial Assistant: Linda Robinson
Typography: Kim Kaczanowski
Staff Artist: David Lenz

ISBN 0-8249-3046-0
The Hershey Logo is a Trademark of Hershey Foods Corporation, Ideals Publishing Corporation, Licensee.

Copyright © MCMLXXXV by
Hershey Foods Corporation.
All rights reserved.
Printed and bound in the
United States of America.

Published by Ideals Publishing Corporation.
Nelson Place at Elm Hill Pike
Nashville, Tennessee 37214-1000

Chocolate Raspberry Indulgence, page 21.
Cover: Regal Chocolate Torte, page 64.

All recipes developed and tested in the HERSHEY Test Kitchens.

INTRODUCTION

HERSHEY'S Time-Less Desserts is designed for modern consumers: young and urban professionals, two income families, busy people interested in elegant or classic dining at home, and the traditional homemaker desiring quality desserts in a short amount of time. This cookbook features an array of exclusive cocoa and chocolate desserts . . . recipes offering both convenience *and* HERSHEY'S quality.

The HERSHEY Test Kitchens have developed these recipes with contemporary lifestyles in mind: mixing and assembling require from only 5 minutes to less than one hour, and in many cases, desserts can be made ahead (these recipes will be indicated by this make ahead symbol *), refrigerated or frozen. Serving sizes for 2 to 6 are included and designed for small families or intimate gatherings. Recipes feature classic combinations — chocolate and fresh fruit, nuts and cream — combined with some convenience products or mixes.

Inspired by HERSHEY'S goodness and a high-tech world, *Time-Less Desserts* offers ''a chocolate escape'' to busy people, an opportunity to entertain family and friends conveniently, with desserts created for now. From ''Chocolate 2 Steps'' to ''Lighter Chocolate Desserts,'' enjoy very special creations from the chapters which follow . . .

GARNISHES

There are many garnishes that are appropriate and appealing with chocolate desserts. Three of the most popular are Chocolate Leaves, Chocolate Curls, and Sweetened Whipped Cream. Instructions for their preparation follow:

CHOCOLATE LEAVES

Wash and thoroughly dry rose or lemon leaves. Melt HERSHEY'S Semi-Sweet or Milk Chocolate Chips in top of double boiler over hot, not boiling, water; stir until completely melted. With small soft-bristled pastry brush, brush melted chocolate on *underside* of each leaf. (The underside provides attractive markings.) Avoid getting chocolate on the front of the leaf; it will make removal difficult. Place coated leaves on wax paper-covered cookie sheet; chill until firm.

Carefully peel the leaves away from the chocolate; do not try to peel the chocolate from the leaves. Cover; chill until ready to use.

CHOCOLATE CURLS

The secret to successful curls is having the chocolate at the proper temperature. It should feel slightly warm but still firm. On a warm day, room temperature might be fine.

To warm, place unwrapped chocolate on a cookie sheet. Place in cooled oven; watch carefully! (Or place in microwave oven on high power for 30 seconds or just until chocolate feels slightly warm.) With even pressure, draw a vegetable peeler along the *underside* of the chocolate, forming a curl. Use a toothpick to lift the curl onto wax paper-covered tray. Continue making curls in this manner. Chill until firm.

For narrow curls, you can use the side of a HERSHEY'S Milk Chocolate or SPECIAL DARK Bar. For short, medium-size curls, use one or two squares of the chocolate bar. For large curls, use the entire width of the bar.

Note: When firm, chocolate curls can be refrigerated in a covered container and stored almost indefinitely.

SWEETENED WHIPPED CREAM

Combine 1 cup heavy or whipping cream, 1 to 2 tablespoons confectioners' sugar, and ½ teaspoon vanilla in small mixer bowl; beat until stiff peaks form. About 2 cups whipped cream.

MELTING HERSHEY'S AND REESE'S PRODUCTS IN THE MICROWAVE OVEN

HERSHEY'S UNSWEETENED BAKING CHOCOLATE AND SEMI-SWEET BAKING CHOCOLATE:

Unwrap blocks, break in half, and place desired amount of HERSHEY'S Unsweetened Baking or Semi-Sweet Baking Chocolate in 1-cup micro-proof measuring cup or small micro-proof bowl. Microwave on high (full power) for minimum time listed below, or until chocolate is softened; stir. Allow to stand several minutes to finish melting; stir again. (If unmelted chocolate still remains, return to microwave on high for additional 30 seconds; stir until fluid.)

1 block (1 ounce)   — 1 to 1½ minutes
2 blocks (2 ounces) — 1½ to 2 minutes
3 blocks (3 ounces) — 2 to 2½ minutes
4 blocks (4 ounces) — 2½ to 3 minutes

HERSHEY'S SEMI-SWEET CHOCOLATE CHIPS, MINI CHIPS, MILK CHOCOLATE CHIPS, AND REESE'S PEANUT BUTTER FLAVORED CHIPS:

Place 1 cup (about 6 ounces) HERSHEY'S Semi-Sweet Chocolate chips, MINI CHIPS, Milk Chocolate Chips or REESE'S Peanut Butter Chips into a 2 cup micro-proof measuring cup or small micro-proof bowl. Microwave on high (full power) for 1 to 1½ minutes, or until softened; stir. Allow to stand several minutes to finish melting. Alternate method: Place 2 cups (about 12 ounces) HERSHEY'S Semi-Sweet Chocolate Chips, MINI CHIPS, Milk Chocolate Chips or REESE'S Peanut Butter Chips into a 4 cup micro-proof measuring cup or medium micro-proof bowl. Microwave on high (full power) for 2 to 2½ minutes; proceed as directed above.

OTHER CHOCOLATE HINTS FOR THE MICROWAVE:

Stirring periodically with a wire whisk while melting, helps blending and prevents scorching.

Overheating chocolate or peanut butter chips when melting, results in scorching and a plastic-like, cohesive mass or "crumbs". If this happens, add one to two tablespoons shortening per six ounces product (do not use butter or margarine); stir until fluid.

Do not allow chocolate to come in contact with a wet spoon or bowl during melting, as this can result in a cohesive or "tight" mass. If this occurs, add shortening as directed above.

Allow for standing time; chocolate products continue to melt after removal from microwave oven.

Melting times for chocolate and confectionery products vary according to amount being melted, size of container used, and composition of the product.

CHOCOLATE 2 STEPS

CHOCOLATE BANANA CREME PIES*

Yield: 3 servings

- **6 tablespoons sugar**
- **1½ tablespoons HERSHEY'S Cocoa**
- **1½ tablespoons cornstarch**
- **¾ cup milk**
- **2 teaspoons butter**
- **1 teaspoon banana-flavored liqueur**
- **1 medium banana, sliced**
- **3 miniature graham cracker tart shells**
  Sweetened whipped cream
  Chocolate curls

Combine sugar, HERSHEY'S Cocoa and cornstarch in small saucepan; gradually add milk, stirring until smooth. Cook over medium heat, stirring constantly, until mixture boils; boil and stir 2 minutes. Remove from heat; stir in butter and liqueur. Pour into bowl; press plastic wrap onto surface. Cool to room temperature. Layer chocolate mixture and several banana slices in tart shells; top with remaining chocolate mixture. Cover; chill until firm. Garnish with sweetened whipped cream, remaining banana slices, and chocolate curls.

DOUBLE CHOCOLATE SWEETHEART PIE*

Yield: about 6 servings

- **4⅛-ounce package *instant* chocolate pudding and pie filling mix**
- **1¾ cups HERSHEY'S Chocolate Milk**
- **6-ounce graham cracker ready pie crust**
  Sweetened whipped cream
  Chocolate curls

Prepare pie filling according to package directions, using HERSHEY'S Chocolate Milk in place of white milk; pour into graham cracker crust. Cover; chill until firm. Serve with sweetened whipped cream and chocolate curls; refrigerate leftovers.

CHOCOLATE CRESCENTS

Yield: 4 servings

- **1 package (8 ounces) refrigerated crescent dinner rolls**
- **2 HERSHEY'S Milk Chocolate Bars (1.45 ounces each)**

Separate dough into 8 triangles. Break each HERSHEY'S Milk Chocolate Bar into 12 pieces (bars are already scored). Place 2 chocolate bar pieces at wide end of each triangle; place 1 additional piece on top. Starting at wide end, roll to opposite point; pinch edges to seal. Place rolls, pointed sides down, on ungreased baking sheet. Bake at 375° for 8 to 10 minutes or until lightly browned. Cool slightly; serve warm.

Chocolate Banana Creme Pies, this page; Hershey's Syrup Pie, page 11.

SUNBURST CHOCOLATE CAKE

Yield: 4 to 6 servings

- **2 tablespoons butter, melted**
- **¼ cup packed light brown sugar**
- **1 tablespoon light corn syrup**
- **3 canned pear halves**
- **4 maraschino cherries, cut into quarters**
- **2 tablespoons pecan pieces**
- **5 tablespoons butter, softened**
- **⅔ cup sugar**
- **½ teaspoon vanilla**
- **1 egg**
- **¾ cup unsifted all-purpose flour**
- **2 tablespoons HERSHEY'S Cocoa**
- **¼ teaspoon baking soda**
- **¼ cup buttermilk** *or* **sour milk***
  Sweetened whipped cream, optional

Combine 2 tablespoons melted butter, the brown sugar and corn syrup in 8½ x 4½ x 2⅝-inch loaf pan; spread evenly over bottom of pan. Drain pear halves; slice each half lengthwise into 4 sections and arrange in sunburst design over mixture in pan. Arrange cherries and pecans between pear sections, in center and at corners.

Cream 5 tablespoons butter, the sugar and vanilla in small mixer bowl. Add egg; beat well. Combine flour, HERSHEY'S Cocoa and baking soda; add alternately with buttermilk or sour milk to creamed mixture.

Carefully pour batter over fruit and nuts in pan. Bake at 350° for 30 to 35 minutes or until cake tester comes out clean. Immediately invert onto serving plate. Serve warm or cold with sweetened whipped cream, if desired.

*To sour milk: Use ¾ teaspoon vinegar plus milk to equal ¼ cup.

CHOCOLATE LADYFINGERS

Yield: 1 dozen ladyfingers

- **3 egg yolks, at room temperature**
- **¼ cup sugar**
- **½ teaspoon vanilla**
- **½ cup plus 1 tablespoon unsifted all-purpose flour**
- **3 tablespoons HERSHEY'S Cocoa**
- **3 egg whites, at room temperature**
- **3 tablespoons sugar**
  Confectioners' sugar

Grease and flour a ladyfinger mold pan. Beat egg yolks, ¼ cup sugar and the vanilla until very thick in small mixer bowl. Combine flour and HERSHEY'S Cocoa in small mixer bowl. Add to yolk mixture 1 tablespoon at a time, with mixer running at low speed. (The mixture will be extremely thick.) Beat egg whites in large mixer bowl until foamy; gradually add 3 tablespoons sugar and beat until stiff peaks form. With mixer on lowest speed, beat one-fourth of egg white mixture into yolks; fold in remaining whites by hand. Fill prepared ladyfinger molds with batter. Sift confectioners' sugar generously over tops of ladyfingers. Bake at 350° for 12 to 15 minutes or until cake tester comes out clean. Cool 5 minutes; invert onto wire rack. Cool completely.

MINI CHIPS PUDDIN' CAKE

Yield: about 6 servings

13.5-ounce package applesauce
   raisin snack cake mix
1½ cups HERSHEY'S MINI CHIPS
   Semi-Sweet Chocolate,
   divided
1⅓ cups packed light brown sugar
1¼ cups water
1 tablespoon lemon juice
1 tablespoon butter *or* margarine
   Sweetened whipped cream

Prepare cake batter according to package directions; stir in ¾ cup HERSHEY'S MINI CHIPS Semi-Sweet Chocolate. Pour into 8-inch square pan. Sprinkle remaining ¾ cup HERSHEY'S MINI CHIPS Semi-Sweet Chocolate evenly over batter in pan; set aside. Combine brown sugar, water, lemon juice and butter or margarine in 2-quart saucepan. Cook over medium heat, stirring constantly, until mixture comes to a full boil. Carefully pour hot mixture over batter in pan. (*Do not stir.*) Bake at 350° for 45 minutes. Let stand 20 to 25 minutes before serving. Serve warm with sweetened whipped cream.

QUICK CHOCOLATE CUPCAKES

Yield: about 8 cupcakes

¾ cup unsifted all-purpose flour
½ cup sugar
2 tablespoons HERSHEY'S Cocoa
½ teaspoon baking soda
¼ teaspoon salt
½ cup water
3 tablespoons vegetable oil
1½ teaspoons vinegar
½ teaspoon vanilla

Combine flour, sugar, HERSHEY'S Cocoa, baking soda and salt in medium mixing bowl. Add water, oil, vinegar and vanilla. Beat with wire whisk just until batter is smooth and ingredients are well blended. Pour batter into paper-lined muffin cups (2½ inches in diameter), filling each ⅔ full. Bake at 375° for 16 to 18 minutes or until tester inserted in center comes out clean. Frost as desired.

CHOCOLATE ALMOND ROLLS

Yield: 4 servings

1 package (8 ounces) refrigerated
   crescent dinner rolls
About ⅓ cup HERSHEY'S Semi-
   Sweet Chocolate Chips
1 tablespoon light corn syrup
1 tablespoon butter, melted
2 tablespoons sliced almonds

Unroll dough; separate into four rectangles. Press seams together with fingers. Place one heaping tablespoon HERSHEY'S Semi-Sweet Chocolate Chips across one narrow end of each rectangle; starting from this end, roll up carefully, pinching ends shut. Place seam side down on ungreased cookie sheet. Bake at 350° for 15 to 20 minutes, or until puffed and golden brown. Remove from oven; brush immediately with corn syrup combined with melted butter. Place sliced almonds evenly over top of rolls; cool on wire rack.

HERSHEY'S SYRUP PIE*

Yield: about 6 servings

2 egg yolks
⅓ cup cornstarch
¼ teaspoon salt
1¾ cups milk
1 cup HERSHEY'S Chocolate Flavored Syrup
1 teaspoon vanilla
6-ounce graham cracker ready pie crust
Sweetened whipped cream
Chocolate curls

Beat egg yolks in a medium micro-proof bowl. Add cornstarch, salt, milk and HERSHEY'S Chocolate Flavored Syrup; blend well. Microwave on medium-high (⅔ power) for 6 to 8 minutes, stirring every 2 minutes with wire whisk or until mixture is smooth and thickened; stir in vanilla. Pour into graham cracker crust. Place plastic wrap directly onto surface of pie; chill several hours or overnight. Garnish with sweetened whipped cream and chocolate curls.

PEANUT BUTTER CREAM PIE*

Yield: 6 servings

1 cup REESE'S Peanut Butter Chips
1 package (3½ ounces) *instant* vanilla pudding mix
1 cup dairy sour cream
1 cup milk
6-ounce graham cracker *or* butter flavored ready pie crust
½ cup heavy or whipping cream
1 tablespoon confectioners' sugar
Fresh fruit

Melt REESE'S Peanut Butter Chips in top of double boiler or in microwave oven; stir until smooth. Remove from heat; set aside. Beat instant pudding mix, sour cream and milk in small mixer bowl; beat in melted peanut butter chips. Pour into crust; chill at least 2 hours. Beat cream and confectioners' sugar until stiff; spread over top of pie. Garnish with fresh fruit.

PEANUT BUTTER TARTS*

Yield: 6 tarts

1 package (3½ ounces) *instant* vanilla pudding and pie filling mix
1½ cups cold milk, divided
1 cup REESE'S Peanut Butter Chips
1 package (4 ounces) miniature graham cracker tart shells
Sweetened whipped cream
Fresh fruit

Beat pudding mix with 1 cup of the milk in small mixer bowl on low speed for about 2 minutes; set aside. Combine REESE'S Peanut Butter Chips with remaining ½ cup milk in top of double boiler over hot water, stirring constantly until blended. Gradually add warm peanut butter mixture to pudding, beating on low speed; beat on medium speed until well blended. Pipe into graham cracker shells. Cover; chill several hours or overnight. Top with sweetened whipped cream and fresh fruit just before serving.

Peanut Butter Tarts, this page.

APPLE AND CHIP COFFEECAKE

Yield: 6 servings

- 1 package (11.5 ounces) spicy apple muffin mix
- ½ cup HERSHEY'S MINI CHIPS Semi-Sweet Chocolate, divided
- 2 tablespoons packed brown sugar
- 1 tablespoon flour
- ¼ teaspoon cinnamon
- 1 tablespoon butter

Prepare muffin mix according to package directions; stir in ¼ cup HERSHEY'S MINI CHIPS Semi-Sweet Chocolate until blended. Spread in greased 8-inch layer pan. Combine brown sugar, flour and cinnamon; cut in butter until mixture is crumbly. Stir in remaining ¼ cup HERSHEY'S MINI CHIPS Semi-Sweet Chocolate. Sprinkle mixture evenly over batter. Bake at 375° for 30 to 35 minutes. Cool.

ROLO CANDIED APPLES*

Yield: 6 coated apples

- 6 wooden sticks
- 6 medium-size apples, stems removed
- 31 ROLO Caramels in Milk Chocolate candies, unwrapped
- 1 tablespoon milk

Insert a wooden stick into stem end of each washed and thoroughly dried apple. Combine ROLO candies with milk in top of double boiler over hot water. Stir until melted. (Add additional milk, several drops at a time, if coating is too thick.) Dip apples into hot ROLO candy mixture; turn until coated. Scrape off excess coating. Place on generously buttered wax paper; chill until firm. Store, covered, in cool place.

OATMEAL CHOCOLATE CHIP COOKIES

Yield: about 2 dozen

- 6 tablespoons butter, softened
- ½ cup packed light brown sugar
- ¼ cup sugar
- 2 tablespoons beaten egg
- ½ teaspoon vanilla
- ½ cup unsifted all-purpose flour
- ¼ teaspoon baking soda
- 2 tablespoons milk
- 1¼ cups quick-cooking oats
- 1 cup HERSHEY'S Semi-Sweet Chocolate Chips

Cream butter, brown sugar, sugar, beaten egg and vanilla in small mixer bowl until light and fluffy. Combine flour and baking soda in small mixing bowl. Add alternately with milk to creamed mixture; beat well. Stir in oats and HERSHEY'S Semi-Sweet Chocolate Chips. Drop by teaspoonfuls onto lightly greased cookie sheets. Bake at 375° for 10 to 12 minutes or until lightly browned. Remove from cookie sheet; cool on wire rack.

Note: Do not use vegetable shortening spray for greasing cookie sheet because cookies will flatten.

CHOCOLATE-CHOCOLATE CHIP COOKIES

Yield: about 1½ dozen

- ¼ cup butter, softened
- ½ cup sugar
- 2 tablespoons beaten egg
- ½ teaspoon vanilla
- ¾ cup unsifted all-purpose flour
- 2½ tablespoons HERSHEY'S Cocoa
- ¼ teaspoon baking soda
- 2 tablespoons milk
- ½ cup HERSHEY'S Semi-Sweet Chocolate Chips

Cream butter, sugar, beaten egg and vanilla in small mixer bowl until light and fluffy. Combine flour, HERSHEY'S Cocoa and baking soda in small mixing bowl. Add alternately with milk to creamed mixture; beat well. Stir in HERSHEY'S Semi-Sweet Chocolate Chips. Drop by teaspoonfuls onto ungreased cookie sheets. Bake at 375° for 10 to 12 minutes or until almost set. Do not overbake. Cool 1 minute on cookie sheet. Remove from cookie sheet; cool completely on wire rack.

CHOCOLATE SLICE & BAKE COOKIES*

Yield: about 1½ dozen

- ¼ cup butter, softened
- ½ cup sugar
- 2 tablespoons beaten egg
- ½ teaspoon vanilla
- ⅔ cup unsifted all-purpose flour
- ¼ cup HERSHEY'S Cocoa
- ¼ plus ⅛ teaspoon baking soda

Cream butter, sugar, beaten egg and vanilla in small mixer bowl until light and fluffy. In a separate bowl, combine flour, HERSHEY'S Cocoa and baking soda; blend into creamed mixture. Shape into 1½-inch thick roll. Wrap in plastic wrap; chill until dough is firm enough to handle. Slice dough ⅛ inch thick. Place on ungreased cookie sheet. Bake at 375° for 8 to 10 minutes or until almost set. Cool slightly on cookie sheet. Remove from cookie sheet; cool completely on wire rack.

CHOCOLATE CHIP WHOLE-WHEAT COOKIES

Yield: 2½ dozen

- ½ cup unsifted whole-wheat flour
- ¼ teaspoon baking soda
- 6 tablespoons shortening
- ¾ cup packed light brown sugar
- 2 tablespoons beaten egg
- 2 tablespoons water
- ½ teaspoon vanilla
- 1 cup quick-cooking oats
- ½ cup chopped dried apricots
- ½ cup HERSHEY'S MINI CHIPS Semi-Sweet Chocolate

Combine whole-wheat flour and baking soda in small mixing bowl; set aside. Cream shortening and brown sugar in small mixer bowl until light and fluffy. Add beaten egg, water and vanilla; beat well. Stir reserved flour mixture into creamed mixture. Stir in oats, dried apricots and HERSHEY'S MINI CHIPS Semi-Sweet Chocolate. Drop mixture by teaspoonfuls onto lightly greased cookie sheets. Flatten slightly. Bake at 350° for 10 to 12 minutes or until golden brown. Remove from cookie sheets. Cool on wire rack.

CHOCOLATE SENTIMENTS

CHRISTMAS KISS KANDIES

Yield: about 12 candies

6 tablespoons slivered almonds
¼ cup confectioners' sugar
2½ teaspoons light corn syrup
½ teaspoon almond extract
   Red food color
   Green food color
12 HERSHEY'S KISSES
   Chocolates, unwrapped
   Sugar

Pour slivered almonds in blender container; cover and blend on high until very finely chopped. Pour into mixing bowl; combine with confectioners' sugar. Combine corn syrup and almond extract; drizzle into almond mixture, stirring until blended. Divide mixture in half. To one half, add several drops red food color; into remaining mixture, add several drops green food color. Mix with hands until colors are well blended and mixture clings together. Shape about one teaspoon almond mixture around each HERSHEY'S KISS candy, keeping the same shape. Roll in sugar. Store in airtight container.

CHOCOLATE THUMBPRINTS

Yield: 26 cookies

½ cup butter *or* margarine
⅔ cup sugar
1 egg yolk
2 tablespoons milk
1 teaspoon vanilla
1 cup unsifted all-purpose flour
¼ cup HERSHEY'S Cocoa
¼ teaspoon salt
1 cup finely chopped nuts
2 tablespoons sugar
1 egg white, slightly beaten
   Vanilla Filling (below)
   Candied cherry, walnut, pecan halves, *or* HERSHEY'S KISSES Chocolates (unwrapped)

Cream butter or margarine, ⅔ cup sugar, egg yolk, milk and vanilla in small mixer bowl. Combine flour, HERSHEY'S Cocoa and salt; blend into creamed mixture. Chill dough about 1 hour or until firm enough to handle. Roll dough into 1-inch balls. Combine chopped nuts and 2 tablespoons sugar in a small bowl. Dip balls of cookie dough into beaten egg white, then into nut mixture. Place on lightly greased cookie sheet. Press thumb gently in center of each cookie. Bake at 350° for 10 to 12 minutes or until set. As soon as cookies are removed from oven, spoon about ¼ teaspoon filling in "thumbprint." Gently place cherry half, walnut, pecan halves, or HERSHEY'S KISS candy in center. Carefully remove from cookie sheet; cool on wire rack.

VANILLA FILLING

Thoroughly combine ½ cup confectioners' sugar, 1 tablespoon butter, 2 tablespoons milk and ¼ teaspoon vanilla in a small bowl.

Chocolate Thumbprints, this page;
Chocolate Spritz Cookies, page 16.

CHOCOLATE SPRITZ COOKIES

Yield: about 2 dozen cookies

- ½ **cup butter, softened**
- ⅓ **cup sugar**
- 1 **tablespoon beaten egg**
- ½ **teaspoon vanilla**
- 1 **cup plus 2 tablespoons unsifted all-purpose flour**
- 2½ **tablespoons HERSHEY'S Cocoa**
- ¼ **teaspoon salt**
  Red candied cherries, optional

Cream butter, sugar, egg and vanilla in small mixer bowl until light and fluffy. Combine flour, HERSHEY'S Cocoa and salt; gradually add to creamed mixture.

Fill cookie press with dough. Press dough onto cool, ungreased cookie sheet. Bake at 350° for 5 to 7 minutes or just until set. Remove from cookie sheet; cool completely on wire rack. Garnish with red candied cherries, if desired.

FILLED CHOCOLATE BARS

Yield: about 12 bars

- ¼ **cup butter** or **margarine**
- 1 **block (1 ounce) HERSHEY'S Unsweetened Baking Chocolate, broken into pieces**
- 1 **egg**
- ½ **cup sugar**
- ¼ **cup unsifted all-purpose flour**
- ⅛ **teaspoon salt**
- ½ **teaspoon vanilla**
- ½ **cup finely chopped nuts**
  MINI CHIPS Glaze (below)
  Sliced almonds
  Vanilla Filling (below)

Melt butter or margarine in small saucepan; remove from heat. Immediately add HERSHEY'S Unsweetened Baking Chocolate; stir until chocolate is melted and mixture is smooth.

Beat egg in small mixer bowl; blend in sugar, flour and salt. Add chocolate mixture and vanilla; blend well. Stir in chopped nuts.

Grease 9-inch square pan; line bottom with wax paper or aluminum foil. Spread batter evenly in pan with spatula. Bake at 400° for 10 to 12 minutes; cool completely. Remove from pan onto cutting board; cut in half crosswise. Spread one half with MINI CHIPS Glaze; sprinkle with sliced almonds. Spread remaining half with Vanilla Filling. Stack with chocolate glazed layer on top. Cut into bars.

MINI CHIPS GLAZE

Bring 2 tablespoons sugar and 1 tablespoon water to boil in a small saucepan. Remove from heat; immediately add ¼ cup HERSHEY'S MINI CHIPS Semi-Sweet Chocolate, stirring until melted and mixture is smooth. Spread while warm.

VANILLA FILLING

Combine ½ cup confectioners' sugar, 1 tablespoon softened butter, 1½ teaspoons milk and ¼ teaspoon vanilla in small mixer bowl; beat until of spreading consistency.

CHOCOLATE COOKIE PRETZELS

Yield: about 12 pretzels or 15 pretzel sticks

1¼ cups unsifted all-purpose flour
¼ cup HERSHEY'S Cocoa
¼ teaspoon baking soda
⅛ teaspoon salt
⅓ cup butter *or* **margarine**
½ cup sugar
1 teaspoon vanilla
1 egg
Confectioners' sugar *or* **Cocoa Glaze (below)**

Combine flour, HERSHEY'S Cocoa, baking soda and salt in small bowl; set aside. Cream butter or margarine, sugar and vanilla in small mixer bowl until light and fluffy. Add egg; beat well. Gradually add dry ingredients to creamed mixture, blending thoroughly. Divide dough into 12 pieces; shape into balls 1½ inches in diameter.

To form twisted pretzels: Roll each piece into a 12-inch rope on lightly-floured surface with hands; place on ungreased cookie sheet. Cross left side of rope over to middle, forming a loop. Fold right side up and over first loop to form pretzel shape; place about 2 inches apart on cookie sheet.

To form pretzel sticks: Roll piece of dough into an 8-inch rope. Bake at 350° for 8 minutes or until set. Cool for 1 minute on cookie sheet; remove to wire rack and cool completely. Sprinkle cookies with confectioners' sugar or frost with Cocoa Glaze.

COCOA GLAZE

⅔ cup confectioners' sugar
1 tablespoon butter
2 tablespoons HERSHEY'S Cocoa
1 tablespoon water
¼ teaspoon vanilla

Measure confectioners' sugar into small mixer bowl; set aside. Melt butter in small saucepan over low heat. Add HERSHEY'S Cocoa and water, stirring constantly, until mixture thickens; do not boil. Remove from heat; add chocolate mixture to confectioners' sugar in mixer bowl. Blend in vanilla; beat until smooth and of spreading consistency.

MINI CHIPS SNACK MIX

Yield: about 1¼ cups

½ cup HERSHEY'S MINI CHIPS
Semi-Sweet Chocolate
¼ cup salted sunflower kernels
¼ cup dry roasted peanuts
¼ cup raisins

Toss ingredients together in small bowl. Store in airtight container.

MINI CHIPS FRUIT MUFFINS

Yield: 12 muffins

1 package (11.5 ounces) banana
    nut muffin mix
⅓ cup chopped dried apricots
⅓ cup HERSHEY'S MINI CHIPS
    Semi-Sweet Chocolate
Butter *or* cream cheese

Prepare muffin mix batter according to package directions; stir in apricots and HERSHEY'S MINI CHIPS Semi-Sweet Chocolate. Grease 12 muffin cups (2½ inches in diameter) on bottom only. Spoon batter into muffin cups, filling each about ½ to ⅔ full. Bake at 400° for 18 to 22 minutes, or until golden brown. Cool slightly; serve warm with butter or cream cheese.

DOUBLE CHOCOLATE TRUFFLES*

Yield: about 2 dozen truffles

½ cup heavy or whipping cream
1 tablespoon sweet butter
4 blocks (4 ounces) HERSHEY'S
    Semi-Sweet Baking
    Chocolate, broken into pieces
1 HERSHEY'S Milk Chocolate Bar
    (4 ounces), broken into pieces
1 tablespoon almond-flavored
    liqueur
Ground almonds

Place heavy cream and sweet butter in small saucepan; cook over medium heat, stirring constantly, just until mixture is very hot. DO NOT BOIL. Remove from heat; stir in HERSHEY'S Semi-Sweet Baking Chocolate pieces, and HERSHEY'S Milk Chocolate Bar pieces and almond-flavored liqueur with wire whisk until smooth. Press plastic wrap over surface; cool several hours or until mixture is firm enough to handle. Roll mixture into 1-inch balls; roll in ground almonds. Chill until mixture is firm enough to handle. Serve cold.

MOCHA TRUFFLES*

Yield: 1½ dozen truffles

¼ cup heavy or whipping cream
3 tablespoons sugar
3 tablespoons sweet *or* regular
    butter
1½ teaspoons instant coffee
    granules
½ cup HERSHEY'S MINI CHIPS
    Semi-Sweet Chocolate
½ teaspoon vanilla
Confectioners' sugar *or*
    HERSHEY'S Semi-Sweet
    Baking Chocolate, grated

Combine heavy cream, sugar, butter and instant coffee granules in small saucepan; cook over low heat, stirring constantly, just until mixture boils. Remove from heat; immediately add HERSHEY'S MINI CHIPS Semi-Sweet Chocolate. Stir until chips are melted and mixture is smooth; add vanilla. Pour into small bowl; chill, stirring occasionally until mixture begins to set. Cover; chill until mixture is firm enough to handle. Form small amounts of chocolate into ½-inch balls, working quickly to prevent melting; roll in confectioners' sugar or grated chocolate. Store, covered, in refrigerator; serve cold.

*Double Chocolate Truffles, this page;
Easy Chocolate Truffles, page 20;
Mocha Truffles, this page.*

EASY CHOCOLATE TRUFFLES*

Yield: about 1½ dozen truffles

¼ cup sweet butter, softened
¼ cup HERSHEY'S Cocoa
1¼ cups confectioners' sugar
2 tablespoons heavy or whipping cream
¾ teaspoon vanilla
After-dinner mints, whole candied cherries, whole almonds, pecan or walnut halves
Confectioners' sugar, flaked coconut or chopped nuts

Cream butter in small mixer bowl. Combine HERSHEY'S Cocoa and confectioners' sugar; add alternately with heavy cream and vanilla to butter. Blend well. Chill until mixture is firm enough to handle. Shape small amount of mixture around mints, candied cherries, almonds, pecans or walnuts for centers; roll into 1-inch balls. Drop into confectioners' sugar, coconut or chopped nuts as coating; turn until well covered. Chill until firm.

VARIATION:

Rum Chocolate Truffles: Add ¼ teaspoon rum extract; decrease vanilla to ½ teaspoon.

CHOCOLATE SHORTBREAD

Yield: about 1½ dozen cookies

½ cup butter, softened
⅔ cup confectioners' sugar
¾ teaspoon vanilla
¼ cup HERSHEY'S Cocoa
¾ cup plus 2 tablespoons unsifted all-purpose flour
Cocoa Glaze (below)

Cream butter, confectioners' sugar and vanilla in small mixer bowl; add HERSHEY'S Cocoa. Gradually blend in flour. Roll or pat out on lightly floured surface to ½-inch thickness. Cut into rectangles (about 2¼ x 1½ inches) with decorative pastry cutter, if available.

Place on ungreased cookie sheet. With a fork, pierce each cookie several times in a decorative pattern, piercing cookie through to bottom. Bake at 300° for 20 to 25 minutes or until firm. Cool slightly. Remove from cookie sheet; cool completely on wire rack. Prepare Cocoa Glaze; drizzle on top of cookies.

COCOA GLAZE

Melt 1 tablespoon butter in small saucepan over low heat; add 1½ tablespoons HERSHEY'S Cocoa and 2 tablespoons water. Cook over low heat, stirring constantly, until mixture thickens; do not boil. Remove from heat. Blend in ¾ cup confectioners' sugar and ¼ teaspoon vanilla; beat until smooth.

CHOCOLATE RASPBERRY INDULGENCE*

Yield: 6 servings

12 blocks (12 ounces) HERSHEY'S Semi-Sweet Baking Chocolate, broken into pieces
¼ cup raspberry-flavored liqueur
6 egg yolks, at room temperature
1 cup sweet butter, cut into 16 pieces
Raspberry Whipped Cream, optional (below)
Chocolate leaves
Fresh raspberries

Butter a 3-cup decorative mold (or line with plastic wrap and butter plastic wrap); set aside. Microwave HERSHEY'S Semi-Sweet Baking Chocolate pieces with raspberry liqueur in a medium micro-proof bowl on high (full power) for 1 to 1½ minutes, or just until chocolate is melted and mixture is smooth when stirred. Whisk in egg yolks, one at a time, and butter pieces until butter is melted and mixture is smooth. (Return to microwave for 30 seconds to 1 minute on high if mixture becomes too cool, but do not boil.) Pour into prepared mold. Cover; refrigerate 6 hours or until set. Just before serving, set mold in warm water for several seconds. Run metal spatula around edge of mold to loosen; invert onto serving plate. Cut into thin slices to serve. Cover and refrigerate remaining portion up to 3 days. Pipe with Raspberry Whipped Cream, if desired; garnish with chocolate leaves and fresh raspberries.

RASPBERRY WHIPPED CREAM

Combine ½ cup heavy or whipping cream, 1 tablespoon confectioners' sugar and 1 teaspoon raspberry-flavored liqueur until stiff.

CHOCOLATE ALMOND TASSIES

Yield: 1 dozen cookies

¼ cup butter, softened
1½ ounces (half of a 3-ounce package) cream cheese, softened
½ cup unsifted all-purpose flour
2 tablespoons beaten egg
⅓ cup packed light brown sugar
¼ cup chopped almonds
¼ cup HERSHEY'S MINI CHIPS Semi-Sweet Chocolate
½ teaspoon almond-flavored liqueur

Combine butter and cream cheese; stir in flour until dough forms a ball. Divide dough into 12 balls, approximately 1 inch in diameter. Press dough onto bottom and up sides of 12 miniature muffin cups (2 inches in diameter); set aside. Combine beaten egg and brown sugar in small bowl; stir in almonds, HERSHEY'S MINI CHIPS Semi-Sweet Chocolate and liqueur. Divide filling among prepared cups. Bake at 350° for 20 to 25 minutes, or until the filling is puffed slightly and pastry is golden brown. Cool; remove from pans by loosening edges.

PECAN TURTLES*

Yield: 12 candies

> 1 cup HERSHEY'S Semi-Sweet
>   Chocolate Chips
> 1 tablespoon shortening
> 6 large marshmallows
> ¾ cup (about 3¼ ounces) pecan
>   halves

Melt HERSHEY'S Semi-Sweet Chocolate Chips and shortening in top of double boiler over hot water; remove from heat. Meanwhile, cut marshmallows in half horizontally; place on wax paper and flatten slightly. Set aside. On wax paper-covered tray, form head and hind feet of turtle by arranging 3 pecan halves with ends touching in center; for front feet, place 1 pecan quarter on each side of head. Arrange 12 of these clusters as bases for turtles. Spoon ½ teaspoon melted mixture into center of each cluster of pecans. To make turtle shell, use a fork to dip each marshmallow half in melted chocolate mixture; place each dipped marshmallow over set of pecan clusters, pressing down slightly. Top with pecan half. Cool completely. Store, covered, in refrigerator.

ROCKY ROAD

Yield: 8 squares

> 1 cup HERSHEY'S Semi-Sweet
>   Chocolate Chips
> 2 tablespoons butter
> 1 tablespoon shortening
> 2½ cups miniature marshmallows
> ¼ cup chopped nuts

Place HERSHEY'S Semi-Sweet Chocolate Chips, butter and shortening in medium micro-proof bowl; microwave on medium (½ power) for 2 to 4 minutes or until chips are softened and mixture is melted and smooth when stirred. Add marshmallows and nuts; blend well. Spread evenly in buttered 8½ x 4½ x 2⅝-inch loaf pan. Cover; chill until firm. Cut into 2-inch squares.

CHOCOLATE SIGHS

Yield: about 15 cookies

> 1 egg white
>   Dash cream of tartar
>   Dash salt
> ⅓ cup sugar
> ½ teaspoon vanilla
> ¼ cup HERSHEY'S MINI CHIPS
>   Semi-Sweet Chocolate

Beat egg white with cream of tartar and salt in small mixer bowl until soft peaks form. Gradually beat in sugar; continue beating until stiff peaks form. Stir in vanilla and HERSHEY'S MINI CHIPS Semi-Sweet Chocolate. Drop by teaspoonfuls onto greased cookie sheet. Place cookies in a preheated 375° oven. Immediately turn off oven; allow cookies to remain until oven has cooled and cookies are dry.

Chocolate Petits Fours, page 24.

CHOCOLATE PARTY MIX

Yield: about 5 cups mix

1½ cups toasted oat *or* corn cereal
    rings
1½ cups bite-size crispy wheat
    squares cereal
  1 cup salted peanuts
  1 cup thin pretzel sticks
  ½ cup raisins
  ¼ cup butter, melted
  2 tablespoons HERSHEY'S Cocoa
  2 tablespoons sugar

Combine cereals, peanuts, pretzels and raisins in medium mixing bowl. Blend butter, cocoa and sugar in small mixing bowl; stir into cereal mixture. Toss until ingredients are well coated. Pour mixture into 13 x 9-inch pan; bake at 250° for 1 hour, stirring every 15 minutes. Cool. Store in airtight container.

CHOCOLATE PETITS FOURS*

Yield: about 1½ dozen petit fours

1 MINI CHIPS Petits Fours Cake *or*
  1 Chocolate Petits Fours Cake,
  (below or next page)
Raspberry *or* apricot jam
Chocolate Petits Fours Glaze
HERSHEY'S MINI CHIPS
  Semi-Sweet Chocolate
Candied fruit pieces
Decorating gels *or* frostings

Prepare either MINI CHIPS or Chocolate Petits Fours Cake. Cut cake into hearts, diamonds, circles or squares (approximately 1½-inch shapes). Sandwich together with a thin layer of raspberry or apricot jam. Place petits fours on wire rack with wax paper or cookie sheet below to catch drips. Cover until ready to glaze. Prepare Chocolate Petits Fours Glaze. Frost by spooning glaze over the cake pieces until entire piece is covered. Allow glaze to set. Decorate with HERSHEY'S MINI CHIPS Semi-Sweet Chocolate and/or candied fruit pieces, or pipe decorations with tubes of glossy decorating gels or frostings. Refrigerate until serving.

MINI CHIPS PETITS FOURS CAKE

⅓ cup butter *or* margarine
⅔ cup sugar
½ teaspoon vanilla
1 egg
1 cup unsifted all-purpose flour
½ plus ⅛ teaspoon baking powder
⅛ teaspoon salt
⅓ cup milk
½ cup HERSHEY'S MINI CHIPS
  Semi-Sweet Chocolate

Line 9-inch square pan with aluminum foil; grease foil. Cream butter or margarine, sugar and vanilla in small mixer bowl until light and fluffy. Add egg; beat well. Combine flour, baking powder and salt; add alternately with milk, beating just until smooth. Stir in HERSHEY'S MINI CHIPS Semi-Sweet Chocolate. Pour batter into prepared pan. Bake at 350° for 15 to 20 minutes. Cool 10 minutes; remove from pan. Remove foil; cool completely. (This cake freezes well).

CHOCOLATE PETITS FOURS CAKE

2 eggs, separated
¼ cup sugar
¼ cup plus 2 tablespoons ground blanched almonds
2½ tablespoons flour
2½ tablespoons HERSHEY'S Cocoa
¼ teaspoon baking soda
⅛ teaspoon salt
2 tablespoons water
½ teaspoon vanilla
⅛ teaspoon almond extract
2 tablespoons sugar

Line 9-inch square pan with aluminum foil; generously grease foil. Set aside. Beat egg yolks in small mixer bowl for 3 minutes on medium speed of mixer. Gradually add ¼ cup sugar and continue beating 2 minutes longer. Combine almonds, flour, HERSHEY'S Cocoa, baking soda and salt; add alternately with water to egg yolk mixture on low speed of mixer, just until blended. Stir in vanilla and almond extract. Beat egg whites in large mixer bowl until foamy; gradually add 2 tablespoons sugar and continue beating until stiff peaks form. Carefully fold chocolate mixture into beaten egg whites. Spread batter evenly into prepared pan. Bake at 375° for 12 to 15 minutes or until top springs back when lightly touched. Cool 5 minutes. Invert onto wire rack; peel off foil. Cool completely.

CHOCOLATE PETITS FOURS GLAZE

1 cup HERSHEY'S MINI CHIPS Semi-Sweet Chocolate
¼ cup sweet butter
2 teaspoons vegetable oil

Melt HERSHEY'S MINI CHIPS Semi-Sweet Chocolate in top of double boiler over hot water. Stir in butter and oil until smooth. Cool slightly, stirring occasionally.

INDIVIDUAL CHOCOLATE FRUITCAKES*

Yield: 1 dozen miniature fruitcakes

⅔ cup red candied cherries, cut in half
½ cup pecan pieces
½ cup golden raisins
¼ cup butter or margarine, softened
½ cup sugar
½ teaspoon vanilla
1 egg
⅓ cup unsifted all-purpose flour
2 tablespoons HERSHEY'S Cocoa
⅛ teaspoon baking powder
3 tablespoons milk
Red candied cherries

Combine cherries, pecans and raisins in small mixing bowl; set aside. Cream butter or margarine, sugar and vanilla in large mixer bowl until light and fluffy. Add egg; beat well. Combine flour, HERSHEY'S Cocoa and baking powder; add alternately with milk to creamed mixture, beating just until blended. Stir in reserved fruit-nut mixture. Fill paper-lined muffin cups (2½ inches in diameter) ¾ full with batter. Bake at 325° for 30 to 35 minutes or until cake tester comes out clean. Cool 10 minutes. Immediately wrap in aluminum foil. Cool completely. Garnish with red candied cherries before serving.

CHOCOLATE CHERRY NUT FUDGE*

Yield: about 2½ dozen pieces

⅔ cup sweetened condensed milk (*NOT* evaporated)
1 cup HERSHEY'S Semi-Sweet Chocolate Chips
¼ cup coarsely chopped almonds
¼ cup chopped candied cherries
½ teaspoon almond extract

Combine sweetened condensed milk and HERSHEY'S Semi-Sweet Chocolate Chips in medium micro-proof bowl. Microwave on high (full power) for 1 to 1½ minutes or until chips are softened and mixture is melted and smooth when stirred. Stir in chopped almonds, cherries and almond extract. Spread evenly in aluminum foil-lined 8½ x 4½ x 2⅝-inch loaf pan. Cover; chill until firm. Cut into 1-inch squares.

CHOCOLATE GREETING OR PLACE CARDS*

Yield: 1 large or 6 small cards

1 cup HERSHEY'S MINI CHIPS Semi-Sweet Chocolate
Decorator's Frosting (below)

Melt HERSHEY'S MINI CHIPS Semi-Sweet Chocolate in top of double boiler over hot water; stir until completely melted. Spread into rectangle, about 4½ x 6 inches, on wax paper-covered cookie sheet; the chocolate should be about ⅛ inch thick. Chill for 5 to 8 minutes or just until chocolate begins to set. With sharp knife, score chocolate into 1 large card or six 1½ x 3-inch place cards. Do not try to separate cards at this time. Cover; chill until firm.

Carefully peel wax paper away from cards. Gently break cards apart at score marks. Place on tray; cover and refrigerate until ready to use.

Remove cards from refrigerator about 10 minutes before decorating. Prepare Decorator's Frosting. Using writing or other decorator's tip, decorate cards with names, messages and/or designs.

DECORATOR'S FROSTING

1½ to 1¾ cups confectioners' sugar
2 tablespoons shortening
1 to 2 tablespoons milk
½ teaspoon vanilla
Food color

Combine all ingredients except food color in small mixer bowl; beat until smooth and of desired consistency. Tint with several drops of food color, blending well.

CREME DE CACAO LIQUEUR*

Yield: about 1 pint liqueur

   ¾ cup sugar
   6 tablespoons water
1½ cups vodka
2½ tablespoons HERSHEY'S Cocoa
   ½ vanilla bean, split

Combine sugar and water in small saucepan; cook over medium heat, stirring occasionally, until mixture boils. Reduce heat to low; simmer, stirring occasionally, until sugar has completely dissolved. Remove from heat; cool to room temperature. Measure ½ cup of the mixture; combine with vodka, HERSHEY'S Cocoa and vanilla bean in clean 1-quart glass container. Cover tightly; keep in cool, dark place; shake vigorously every 2 days.

Strain liqueur through dampened coffee filter paper into clean glass container. (Change filter paper in mid-process or, if necessary, let drip overnight as cocoa residue is very thick.) Repeat straining process if residue remains. Remove vanilla bean. Cover tightly; let liqueur age in cool, dark place for at least 1 month.

CHOCOLATE AMARETTO SQUARES

Yield: 16 squares

   ½ cup butter, melted
   6 tablespoons HERSHEY'S Cocoa
   1 cup sugar
   2 eggs
   2 tablespoons almond-flavored
      liqueur
1¼ cups whole almonds
      Sliced almonds, optional

Combine melted butter and HERSHEY'S Cocoa in medium mixing bowl; stir until smooth. Stir in sugar, eggs and almond liqueur. Grind almonds finely in food processor or blender; stir into chocolate mixture. Pour into greased 8-inch square pan. Bake at 325° for 35 to 40 minutes, or just until set. Cool in pan on wire rack. Cut into squares; garnish with sliced almonds, if desired.

CHOCOLATE-CHIP SHORTBREAD

Yield: about 1½ dozen squares

   ½ cup butter, softened
   ¼ cup sugar
1¼ cups unsifted all-purpose flour
   1 teaspoon brandy extract
   ½ teaspoon rum extract
   ½ cup HERSHEY'S MINI CHIPS
      Semi-Sweet Chocolate

Cream butter and sugar in small mixer bowl until light and fluffy. Add flour and extracts; blend well. Stir in HERSHEY'S MINI CHIPS Semi-Sweet Chocolate. Pat into greased 9-inch square pan. Bake at 350° for 30 to 35 minutes or until golden brown. Cool 10 minutes; cut into squares. Glaze, if desired.

HONEY CHOCOLATE BROWNIES

Yield: about 16 brownies

⅓ cup butter *or* margarine, softened
½ cup sugar
2 teaspoons vanilla
⅓ cup honey
2 eggs
½ cup unsifted all-purpose flour
⅓ cup HERSHEY'S Cocoa
½ teaspoon salt
⅔ cup chopped nuts

Cream butter or margarine, sugar and vanilla in large mixer bowl; blend in honey. Add eggs; beat well. Combine flour, HERSHEY'S Cocoa and salt; gradually add to creamed mixture. Stir in nuts. Pour into greased 9-inch square pan. Bake at 350° for 25 to 30 minutes or until brownie begins to pull away from edges of pan. Cool; frost, if desired. Cut into squares.

BAKED BOSTON BROWN BREAD

Yield: 4 loaves

1 package (12 ounces) corn muffin mix
¼ cup HERSHEY'S Cocoa
3 tablespoons flour
2 tablespoons packed light brown sugar
1¼ cups milk
¾ cup chopped nuts
¾ cup raisins
¼ cup dark corn syrup
1 egg, beaten
Butter, margarine *or* cream cheese

Combine corn muffin mix, HERSHEY'S Cocoa, flour and brown sugar in large mixing bowl. Add milk, stirring until dry ingredients are moistened; allow to stand 5 minutes. Stir in nuts, raisins, dark corn syrup and egg. Divide batter equally among four well-greased miniature loaf pans (3¼ x 5¾ x 2¼ inches). Bake at 350° for 35 to 40 minutes or until cake tester inserted comes out clean. Cool 5 minutes; remove from pans. Cool slightly. Slice; serve warm with butter, margarine or cream cheese. (Loaves can be wrapped and frozen.)

HOMEMADE HOT COCOA MIX

Yield: 2¼ cups mix (nine 6-ounce servings)

1¼ cups nonfat dry milk powder
½ cup sugar
¼ cup HERSHEY'S Cocoa
¼ cup non-dairy coffee creamer

Combine nonfat dry milk powder, sugar, HERSHEY'S Cocoa and coffee creamer; blend well. Store in tightly-covered container in cool, dry place.

One serving: Place ¼ cup dry mix in cup; add 6 ounces boiling water. Stir well. Makes one 6-ounce serving.

Four servings: Place 1 cup dry mix in pitcher; add 3 cups boiling water. Stir well. Makes four 6-ounce servings.

CHOCOLATE AND COMPANY

CHOCOLATE CREPES*

Yield: about 18 crepes

- **3 eggs**
- **1 cup unsifted all-purpose flour**
- **2 tablespoons HERSHEY'S Cocoa**
- **2 tablespoons sugar**
- **1¼ cups buttermilk**
- **3 tablespoons butter, melted**
  Peach, Cherry or **Apple pie filling**
  Chocolate Sauce (below)
  Sweetened whipped cream
  Sifted HERSHEY'S Cocoa

Beat eggs in small mixer bowl. Combine flour, HERSHEY'S Cocoa and sugar; add to eggs alternately with buttermilk, beating until smooth. Beat in butter; chill. Heat a small skillet or crepe pan (7 inches in diameter) over medium heat; brush lightly with melted butter. For each crepe, pour about 2 tablespoons batter in pan; immediately rotate pan to evenly cover bottom. Cook about 1 minute; turn and cook on other side. Turn out and cool on wire rack; stack between layers of wax paper. Refrigerate or freeze for later use.

Just before serving, place 2 tablespoons pie filling in center of crepe; fold edges over the filling. Place in a shallow oven-proof dish; heat in oven at 225° for 15 minutes. Drizzle with Chocolate Sauce. Top with a dollop of sweetened whipped cream. Garnish with sprinkling of HERSHEY'S Cocoa.

CHOCOLATE SAUCE

- **¾ cup sugar**
- **⅓ cup HERSHEY'S Cocoa**
- **¾ cup evaporated milk**
- **¼ cup butter**
- **⅛ teaspoon salt**
- **1 teaspoon vanilla**

Combine sugar and HERSHEY'S Cocoa in small saucepan; blend in evaporated milk, butter and salt. Cook over medium heat, stirring constantly, until mixture boils. Remove from heat; stir in vanilla. Serve warm. Cover and refrigerate leftover sauce.

CHOCOLATE CREAM CHEESE SPREAD*

Yield: about 1 cup spread

- **1 package (8 ounces) cream cheese, softened**
- **¼ cup HERSHEY'S Chocolate Flavored Syrup**
- **2 teaspoons HERSHEY'S Cocoa**

Beat cream cheese, HERSHEY'S Chocolate Flavored Syrup and HERSHEY'S Cocoa in small bowl until smooth. Cover; chill several hours or overnight. Serve on crackers.

Chocolate Crepes, this page.

CHOCOLATE LOVER'S CHEESECAKE*

Yield: 6 servings

- **2 packages (8 ounces each) cream cheese, softened**
- **½ cup sugar**
- **2 eggs**
- **1 teaspoon vanilla**
- **1 cup HERSHEY'S MINI CHIPS Semi-Sweet Chocolate**
- **6-ounce graham cracker ready pie crust**
- **Chocolate Topping (below)**

Blend cream cheese and sugar in small mixer bowl. Add eggs and vanilla; beat well. Stir in HERSHEY'S MINI CHIPS Semi-Sweet Chocolate; pour into crust. Bake at 450° for 10 minutes; without opening door, reduce temperature to 250°. Continue to bake for 20 to 25 minutes or just until set. Cool completely. Cover; chill thoroughly. Spread top with Chocolate Topping. Chill several minutes or just until set. Cut into wedges; serve cold.

CHOCOLATE TOPPING

Place ⅓ cup HERSHEY'S MINI CHIPS Semi-Sweet Chocolate and 2 tablespoons heavy or whipping cream in small micro-proof bowl or cup. Microwave on high (full power) for 20 to 30 seconds, or just until chocolate is melted and mixture is smooth when stirred. Cool slightly.

INDIVIDUAL CHOCOLATE CREAM PIES*

Yield: 6 servings

- **1½ ounces (½ of a 3-ounce package) cream cheese, softened**
- **6 tablespoons sugar**
- **½ teaspoon vanilla**
- **2½ tablespoons HERSHEY'S Cocoa**
- **2½ tablespoons milk**
- **1 cup heavy or whipping cream**
- **Six (4-ounce package) miniature graham cracker tart shells**
- **Chocolate Syrup Whipped Cream (below)**

Combine cream cheese, sugar and vanilla in small mixer bowl until blended. Add HERSHEY'S Cocoa alternately with milk, beating until smooth. Whip heavy cream until stiff; fold into chocolate mixture. Spoon into tart shells. Cover; chill until firm. Garnish with Chocolate Syrup Whipped Cream.

CHOCOLATE SYRUP WHIPPED CREAM

- **½ cup heavy or whipping cream**
- **¼ cup HERSHEY'S Chocolate Flavored Syrup**
- **1 tablespoon confectioners' sugar**
- **¼ teaspoon vanilla**

Combine heavy cream, HERSHEY'S Chocolate Flavored Syrup, confectioners' sugar and vanilla in small mixer bowl; beat until soft peaks form. Serve as topping for cakes or other desserts.

CHIFFON-FILLED CHOCOLATE PETAL TARTS*

Yield: 6 servings

Chocolate Petal Tarts (below)
1 teaspoon unflavored gelatine
2 tablespoons cold water
½ cup sugar
3 tablespoons HERSHEY'S Cocoa
⅔ cup milk
1 egg, separated
½ cup heavy or whipping cream, whipped

Prepare Chocolate Petal Tarts; set aside. Sprinkle gelatine onto water in custard cup; let stand 3 to 4 minutes to soften. Combine sugar and HERSHEY'S Cocoa in small saucepan; stir in milk and egg yolk. Cook over low heat, stirring constantly, until mixture thickens; DO NOT BOIL. Remove from heat; stir in gelatine until dissolved. Cool slightly; chill until slightly thickened. Beat egg white until stiff; fold into chocolate with whipped cream. Pour into Chocolate Petal Tarts. Chill until set.

CHOCOLATE PETAL TARTS

1 package (10 ounces) pie crust mix (for 2-crust pie)
2 tablespoons sugar
⅓ cup HERSHEY'S Chocolate Flavored Syrup

Combine pie crust mix and sugar in medium mixing bowl; drizzle with HERSHEY'S Chocolate Flavored Syrup. Mix until smooth. Shape into 2-inch diameter roll. Wrap with plastic wrap; chill until firm. Cut into ¼-inch slices. Place one dough circle in bottom of each of 6 tart pans; place 4 circles around sides of pan. Repeat for 6 pans. Bake at 350° for 15 to 20 minutes or just until set. Cool. Gently remove with knife.

CHOCOLATE CINNAMON DESSERT

Yield: 6 servings

1⅓ cups buttermilk baking mix
¾ cup sugar
⅓ cup HERSHEY'S Cocoa
½ teaspoon cinnamon
3 tablespoons butter or margarine, softened
¾ cup milk
1 egg
2 cups (1 pint) vanilla ice cream
Chocolate Cinnamon Sauce (below)

Combine buttermilk baking mix, sugar, HERSHEY'S Cocoa, cinnamon, butter or margarine, ¼ cup milk and the egg in large mixer bowl; beat 1 minute on medium speed. Add remaining ½ cup milk; blend well. Pour batter into greased and floured 8-inch square pan. Bake at 350° for 30 to 35 minutes or until cake tester inserted comes out clean. Cool; cut into pieces. Serve warm or cold topped with ice cream and Chocolate Cinnamon Sauce.

CHOCOLATE CINNAMON SAUCE

Combine 1 cup HERSHEY'S Chocolate Flavored Syrup and ¼ teaspoon cinnamon in small mixing bowl until well blended.

CHOCOLATE PEACH SHORTCAKE*

Yield: 6 servings

2 eggs, separated
¼ cup sugar
¼ cup unsifted all-purpose flour
3 tablespoons HERSHEY'S Cocoa
2 tablespoons sugar
¼ teaspoon baking soda
3 tablespoons water
2 tablespoons sugar
1 cup heavy or whipping cream
⅓ cup confectioners' sugar
½ teaspoon vanilla
2 cups (16-ounce can) sliced peaches, well drained

Grease bottom of 9-inch square pan; line with wax paper and grease paper. Beat 2 egg yolks 3 minutes on medium speed. Gradually add ¼ cup sugar; continue beating 2 minutes. Combine flour, HERSHEY'S Cocoa, 2 tablespoons sugar and the baking soda; add alternately with water on low speed just until batter is smooth. Beat egg whites until foamy; add 2 tablespoons sugar and beat until stiff peaks form. Carefully fold beaten egg whites into chocolate mixture. Spread batter evenly into prepared pan. Bake at 375° for 12 to 14 minutes or until top springs back when touched lightly. Cool 10 minutes; remove from pan and remove wax paper. Cool completely; chill while preparing filling.

Beat cream, confectioners' sugar and vanilla in large mixer bowl until stiff. Cut cake layer in half horizontally. Place 1 cake layer upside down on serving plate; frost with about 1 cup whipped cream. With decorator's tube or spoon, make a ring of whipped cream ½ inch high and 1 inch wide around edge of layer. Fill center with peach slices, reserving several peach slices for top of cake. Carefully place second layer, top side up, on filling. Gently spread whipped cream on top of cake. With decorator's tube or spoon, make border of whipped cream around edge of top layer of cake. Arrange remaining peach slices in center. Chill until serving.

Chocolate Peach Shortcake, this page.

CHOCOLATE BOURBON PIE

Yield: 6 servings

¼ cup butter, softened
1 egg, beaten
1 teaspoon vanilla or 1 tablespoon bourbon
½ cup sugar
¼ cup unsifted all-purpose flour
½ cup HERSHEY'S MINI CHIPS Semi-Sweet Chocolate
½ cup finely chopped pecans
6-ounce butter-flavored ready pie crust
Sweetened whipped cream

Cream butter in small mixer bowl; add egg and vanilla or bourbon. Combine sugar and flour; add to creamed mixture. Stir in HERSHEY'S MINI CHIPS Semi-Sweet Chocolate and pecans. Pour into pie crust. Bake at 350° for 30 to 35 minutes or until golden brown. Cool slightly; serve warm. Garnish with sweetened whipped cream, if desired.

CHOCOLATE MINT DELIGHT*

Yield: 4 to 6 servings

1 package (3 ounces) lime-flavored gelatine
1 cup boiling water
2 cups (1 pint) vanilla ice cream
½ teaspoon peppermint extract
½ cup HERSHEY'S MINI CHIPS Semi-Sweet Chocolate
Sweetened whipped cream
Additional HERSHEY'S MINI CHIPS Semi-Sweet Chocolate

Dissolve lime gelatine in boiling water. Add ice cream by spoonfuls; stir until melted. Add peppermint extract and HERSHEY'S MINI CHIPS Semi-Sweet Chocolate. Chill about 15 minutes, stirring occasionally, until mixture begins to set. Spoon into dessert dishes; cover and chill until firm. Garnish with sweetened whipped cream and additional HERSHEY'S MINI CHIPS Semi-Sweet Chocolate.

PALM BEACH BROWNIES

Yield: about 16 brownies

½ cup sugar
¼ cup evaporated milk
¼ cup butter or margarine
8 blocks (8 ounces) HERSHEY'S Semi-Sweet Baking Chocolate, broken into pieces
2 eggs
1 teaspoon vanilla
¾ cup unsifted all-purpose flour
¼ teaspoon baking soda
¼ teaspoon salt
¾ cup chopped nuts, optional

Combine sugar, evaporated milk and butter or margarine in medium saucepan. Cook over medium heat, stirring occasionally, until mixture comes to a full rolling boil. Remove from heat; add chocolate, stirring until melted. Beat in eggs and vanilla. Add flour, baking soda and salt; mix until smooth. Stir in nuts, if desired. Pour into greased 9-inch square pan. Bake at 325° for 30 to 35 minutes or until brownie begins to pull away from edges of pan. Cool; frost, if desired. Cut into squares.

CHOCOLATE COATED STRAWBERRIES

Yield: about 6 coated berries

1 cup HERSHEY'S Semi-Sweet Chocolate Chips
1½ teaspoons shortening
1 cup large strawberries, with stems, washed and chilled

Melt HERSHEY'S Semi-Sweet Chocolate Chips and shortening in top of double boiler over hot water; stir until smooth. Holding each berry by stem or hull, dip berry about ⅔ of the way into chocolate mixture. Shake gently to remove excess chocolate. Place dipped berries on wax paper-covered plate or tray; allow chocolate to harden slightly, about 30 minutes.

FUDGE PECAN PIES

Yield: 6 servings

¼ cup sugar
3 tablespoons HERSHEY'S Cocoa
3 tablespoons flour
⅔ cup light corn syrup
1 egg
1½ tablespoons butter, melted
¾ teaspoon vanilla or bourbon
¼ cup chopped pecans
Six (4-ounce package) miniature graham cracker tart shells
Pecan halves
Bourbon Whipped Cream (below)

Combine sugar, HERSHEY'S Cocoa, flour, corn syrup, egg, melted butter and vanilla or bourbon in small mixer bowl; beat 30 seconds on medium speed (do not overbeat). Stir in chopped pecans.

Pour into tart shells. Bake at 350° for 20 to 25 minutes, or just until set; immediately arrange pecan halves on top. Cool. Serve with Bourbon Whipped Cream.

BOURBON WHIPPED CREAM

Whip ½ cup heavy or whipping cream, 1 tablespoon confectioners' sugar and 2 teaspoons bourbon until stiff.

CHOCOLATE DIPPING SAUCE

Yield: about ¾ cup sauce

¼ cup butter or margarine
¼ cup HERSHEY'S Cocoa
½ cup sugar
¼ cup light cream
1 tablespoon cherry-flavored liqueur
Fresh strawberries, banana pieces, apple slices, and dried apricots

Melt butter or margarine in small saucepan over low heat. Remove from heat; immediately stir in HERSHEY'S Cocoa. Add sugar and light cream; cook over low heat, stirring constantly, until sugar is dissolved and mixture is smooth. Remove from heat; stir in cherry-flavored liqueur. Serve while warm with a selection of fruits for dipping.

CHOCOLATE ENCORES

COLD CHOCOLATE SOUFFLÉS*

Yield: 4 servings

1 envelope unflavored gelatine
¼ cup cold water
3 egg yolks
6 tablespoons milk
1½ tablespoons butter
¾ cup HERSHEY'S Chocolate
    Flavored Syrup
2 tablespoons rum
¾ teaspoon vanilla
3 egg whites
⅛ teaspoon cream of tartar
3 tablespoons sugar
½ cup heavy or whipping cream,
    whipped

Measure lengths of aluminum foil to go around 4 ramekins; fold in half lengthwise. Lightly oil one side of each collar; tape securely to outside of dish (oiled side in) allowing collars to extend 1 inch above rim of dish. Set aside.

Sprinkle gelatine onto cold water in small bowl; let stand 5 minutes to soften. Slightly beat egg yolks in medium micro-proof bowl; add milk, gelatine mixture and butter. Microwave on medium-high (⅔ power) for 3 to 4 minutes, stirring once, just until mixture is very hot and coats a spoon. DO NOT BOIL. Blend in HERSHEY'S Chocolate Flavored Syrup, rum and vanilla. Press plastic wrap onto surface. Cool slightly; chill, stirring occasionally, until mixture mounds from spoon.

Beat egg whites with cream of tartar in small mixer bowl until foamy; gradually add sugar, beating until stiff peaks form. Fold egg whites into chocolate mixture. Whip heavy cream until stiff; fold into chocolate mixture. Pour into prepared soufflé dishes; cover and chill until firm. Just before serving, carefully remove foil collars.

QUICK GRAND MARNIER MOUSSE*

Yield: 6 servings

1 cup HERSHEY'S MINI CHIPS
    Semi-Sweet Chocolate
5 tablespoons boiling water
3 eggs, separated
1½ tablespoons Grand Marnier
    liqueur
    Dash cream of tartar
¼ cup sugar
    Sweetened whipped cream

Blend HERSHEY'S MINI CHIPS Semi-Sweet Chocolate in food processor until finely chopped. Sprinkle boiling water over chips; process until smooth. Add egg yolks and liqueur; blend until smooth. Beat egg whites with cream of tartar in small mixer bowl until foamy; gradually add sugar, beating until stiff peaks form. Gently fold chocolate mixture into egg white mixture. Divide among 6 dessert dishes. Cover; chill until firm. Serve topped with sweetened whipped cream.

"Pudding" Chocolate Cheesecake, page 40.

"PUDDING" CHOCOLATE CHEESECAKE*

Yield: 6 servings

Chocolate Crust (below)
1 cup HERSHEY'S MINI CHIPS
Semi-Sweet Chocolate
1 package (8 ounces) cream
cheese, softened
½ cup sugar
4 eggs, at room temperature
¼ cup heavy or whipping cream
1 tablespoon vanilla
Whipped Cream Topping (below)
Orange slices
Orange rind slivers

Prepare Chocolate Crust as directed; set aside. Melt HERSHEY'S MINI CHIPS Semi-Sweet Chocolate in top of double boiler or in microwave oven; stir until smooth. Cool slightly. Beat cream cheese and sugar until light and fluffy. Add eggs, one at a time, beating well after each addition. Beat in reserved chocolate, the heavy cream and vanilla. Pour into crust. Bake at 375° for 30 to 35 minutes or until outside is firm, but center is still soft. Cool to room temperature; chill thoroughly. Remove cake from pan. Prepare Whipped Cream Topping; pipe around edge of cheesecake in decorative design. Garnish with orange slices and orange rind slivers.

CHOCOLATE CRUST

⅓ cup butter
⅓ cup HERSHEY'S MINI CHIPS
Semi-Sweet Chocolate
1 cup dry bread crumbs
⅓ cup sugar

Melt butter and HERSHEY'S MINI CHIPS Semi-Sweet Chocolate over very low heat in small saucepan; stir until smooth. Stir in bread crumbs and sugar. Press onto bottom and up sides of 9-inch layer pan with removable bottom.

WHIPPED CREAM TOPPING

¾ cup heavy or whipping cream
2 tablespoons confectioners' sugar
¼ teaspoon vanilla

Beat heavy cream, confectioners' sugar and vanilla until stiff in small mixer bowl.

HERSHEY BAR PIES*

Yield: 6 servings

1 HERSHEY'S Milk Chocolate Bar
(4 ounces)
2½ tablespoons milk
¾ cup miniature marshmallows
½ cup heavy or whipping cream
Six (4-ounce package) miniature
graham cracker tart shells
Sweetened whipped cream
Chocolate curls

Break HERSHEY'S Milk Chocolate Bar into pieces; combine with milk in top of double boiler over hot water. Stir until chocolate is melted and mixture is smooth. Add marshmallows, stirring until melted; cool completely. Whip heavy cream until stiff; fold into chocolate mixture. Divide evenly among 6 tart shells. Cover; chill several hours until firm. Garnish with sweetened whipped cream and chocolate curls.

LIQUEUR CHOCOLATE CUPS*

Yield: about 9 cups

1 cup HERSHEY'S Semi-Sweet Chocolate Chips
1 teaspoon shortening (*not* butter, margarine or oil)
Liqueur

Melt HERSHEY'S Semi-Sweet Chocolate Chips and shortening in top of double boiler over hot water; remove from heat. Cool slightly.

Place 9 paper candy cups (1½ inches in diameter) in miniature muffin pans. Using a narrow, soft-bristled pastry brush, thickly and evenly coat inside pleated surface and bottom of each cup. Chill coated cups 10 minutes or until set; coat any thin spots again. (If necessary, chocolate mixture may be reheated over hot water.) Cover tightly; chill until very firm, about 1 hour. Carefully peel paper from each cup. Cover and chill at least 1 hour. Fill chilled cups with about 1½ teaspoons of your favorite liqueur.

CHOCOLATE CUPS WITH STRAWBERRY CREAM*

Yield: 4 servings

1 cup HERSHEY'S MINI CHIPS Semi-Sweet Chocolate
Strawberry Cream Filling (below)
Fresh strawberries for garnish

Place HERSHEY'S MINI CHIPS Semi-Sweet Chocolate in top of double boiler over simmering water; stir constantly until melted. Remove from heat; cool slightly. With a soft pastry brush, coat inside pleated surfaces and bottoms of 4 paper-lined muffin cups (2½ inches in diameter) with melted chocolate. Chill 10 minutes; coat any thin spots again. Chill thoroughly. Remove from refrigerator; gently peel off paper. Cover; store in refrigerator. Prepare Strawberry Cream Filling; spoon into chocolate cups. Cover; chill until set. Garnish with fresh strawberries.

STRAWBERRY CREAM FILLING

½ cup heavy or whipping cream
½ cup sliced sweetened strawberries
1 to 2 tablespoons confectioners' sugar
Red food color, optional

Whip heavy cream in small mixer bowl until stiff peaks form. Drain strawberries; purée or mash to equal ¼ cup pulp. Fold into cream; add confectioners' sugar and 1 to 2 drops red food color, if desired.

ALMOND MOCHA CREAM TORTE*

Yield: 6 servings

4 eggs
¾ cup sugar
1 cup slivered almonds
2 tablespoons flour
2½ teaspoons baking powder
Mocha Frosting (below)
Grated chocolate

Line the bottoms of two buttered 8-inch layer pans with wax paper; butter paper. Blend eggs and sugar until smooth in blender container. Add almonds; blend until almonds are finely ground. Add flour and baking powder; blend just until combined. Pour the batter into prepared pans; bake at 350° for 10 to 15 minutes or until layers are golden brown and firm to touch. Cool 5 minutes; invert layers onto wire racks. Remove wax paper; cool completely. Prepare Mocha Frosting. Place one cake layer on serving plate; spread with about ½ cup of frosting. Place second layer on top. Spread remaining frosting on top and sides of torte, covering completely. Cover; chill thoroughly. Cut into slices; serve cold, topped with grated chocolate, if desired.

MOCHA FROSTING

1½ cups heavy or whipping cream
½ cup sugar
¼ cup HERSHEY'S Cocoa
2 teaspoons instant coffee granules
1 tablespoon vanilla

Combine heavy cream, sugar, HERSHEY'S Cocoa, instant coffee and vanilla in blender container. Blend on low speed until stiff; scraping sides of container occasionally.

CHOCOLATE BANANA PARFAITS*

Yield: 4 servings

¾ cup sugar
3 tablespoons HERSHEY'S Cocoa
3 tablespoons cornstarch
1½ cups milk
1½ tablespoons butter
¾ teaspoon vanilla
1 medium banana, sliced
Banana Whipped Cream (below)

Combine sugar, HERSHEY'S Cocoa and cornstarch in small saucepan; gradually add milk, stirring until smooth. Cook over medium heat, stirring constantly, until mixture boils; boil and stir 2 minutes. Remove from heat; stir in butter and vanilla. Pour into bowl; press plastic wrap onto surface. Cool to room temperature. Layer chocolate mixture, banana slices and Banana Whipped Cream in 4 parfait glasses. Chill until firm.

BANANA WHIPPED CREAM

Beat ½ cup heavy or whipping cream, 1 tablespoon confectioners' sugar and 1 tablespoon banana-flavored liqueur until stiff.

Mocha-Filled Cream Puffs, page 44.

43

MOCHA-FILLED CREAM PUFFS*

Yield: about 3 cream puffs

¼ cup water
2 tablespoons butter
¼ cup unsifted all-purpose flour
1 egg
  Mocha Cream Filling (below)
  Confectioners' sugar

Heat water and butter to rolling boil in small saucepan. Add flour all at once; stir vigorously over low heat about 1 minute or until mixture leaves side of pan and forms a ball. Remove from heat. Add egg, beating until smooth and velvety.

Drop by scant ¼ cupfuls onto ungreased cookie sheet. Bake at 400° for 35 to 40 minutes or until puffed and golden brown. While puff is warm, horizontally slice off small portion of top; reserve tops. Remove any soft filaments of dough; cool. Prepare Mocha Cream Filling; fill puffs. Replace tops; dust with confectioners' sugar. Chill; serve cold.

MOCHA CREAM FILLING

⅔ cup sugar
3 tablespoons HERSHEY'S Cocoa
3 tablespoons cornstarch
1½ cups milk
2 to 3 teaspoons instant coffee granules
1 egg yolk, slightly beaten
1 tablespoon butter
½ teaspoon vanilla

Combine sugar, HERSHEY'S Cocoa and cornstarch in medium saucepan; stir in milk and instant coffee granules. Cook over medium heat, stirring constantly, until mixture boils; boil and stir 1 minute. Remove from heat. Gradually stir small amount of chocolate mixture into egg yolk; blend well. Return egg mixture to pan; stir and heat just until boiling. Remove from heat; blend in butter and vanilla. Pour into bowl; press plastic wrap onto surface. Cool.

CHOCOLATE CREAM TARTLETS*

Yield: 6 servings

½ cup sugar
2 tablespoons HERSHEY'S Cocoa
2 tablespoons cornstarch
1½ cups milk
1 egg yolk, slightly beaten
1 tablespoon butter
¼ to ½ teaspoon almond extract
Six (4-ounce package) miniature graham cracker tart shells
  Sweetened whipped cream

Combine sugar, HERSHEY'S Cocoa and cornstarch in small saucepan; add milk and egg yolk. Cook over medium heat, stirring constantly, until mixture boils; boil and stir 1 minute. Remove from heat; blend in butter and almond extract. Pour into tart shells. Cover with plastic wrap; chill. Garnish with sweetened whipped cream and sliced almonds, if desired.

BANANAS FOSTER WITH CHOCOLATE RUM SAUCE

Yield: 4 servings

- 2 tablespoons butter
- 4 teaspoons brown sugar
- 2 large ripe bananas
- 1/8 teaspoon cinnamon
- 2 tablespoons rum *or* brandy
  Ice cream
  Chocolate Rum Sauce (below)

Melt butter in small, heavy skillet; stir in brown sugar. Cut bananas in half lengthwise and then in thirds crosswise; add to skillet mixture and cook, stirring occasionally, just until tender. Sprinkle with cinnamon and rum or brandy; do not stir. Set aflame and spoon over individual portions of ice cream while still flaming. Top with Chocolate Rum Sauce.

CHOCOLATE RUM SAUCE

- 3 tablespoons HERSHEY'S Cocoa
- 1/2 cup sugar
- 1/3 cup evaporated milk
- 2 tablespoons butter
- 1 tablespoon rum
- 1/4 teaspoon vanilla

Combine HERSHEY'S Cocoa and sugar in small saucepan; stir in milk and butter. Cook over low heat, stirring constantly, until mixture boils. Remove from heat; stir in rum and vanilla.

RUM CAKE WITH CHOCOLATE RUM FROSTING*

Yield: 4 servings

- 1 package (16 ounces) golden pound cake mix with vegetable shortening
- 4 tablespoons rum
- 2 tablespoons butter
- 2 blocks (2 ounces) HERSHEY'S Unsweetened Baking Chocolate, broken into pieces
- 2 cups confectioners' sugar
- 1/3 cup milk
- 2 teaspoons rum

Prepare pound cake mix according to package directions, baking in two loaf pans (8½ x 4½ x 2⅝ inches). Cool completely. (Wrap and freeze one cake for later use.)

Trim rounded portion from top of remaining cake and discard. Invert on serving plate; cut into 3 equal layers. Sprinkle bottom and middle layers with 2 tablespoons rum each.

Melt butter in small saucepan; add HERSHEY'S Unsweetened Baking Chocolate pieces. Cook over very low heat, stirring constantly, until chocolate is melted and mixture is smooth. Pour into small mixer bowl. Add confectioners' sugar, milk and 2 teaspoons rum; beat to spreading consistency until well blended. Spread between layers and on top and sides of cake. Chill.

BASIC BLACK

LAS VEGAS CUPCAKES

Yield: about 8 cupcakes

- ¾ cup unsifted all-purpose flour
- ½ cup sugar
- 2 tablespoons HERSHEY'S Cocoa
- ½ teaspoon baking soda
- ¼ teaspoon salt
- ½ cup water
- 3 tablespoons vegetable oil
- 1½ teaspoons vinegar
- ½ teaspoon vanilla
- 2 SKOR Toffee Candy Bars (1.25 ounces each), chopped*
- Las Vegas Frosting (below)
- Additional SKOR Toffee Candy Bar pieces

Combine flour, sugar, HERSHEY'S Cocoa, baking soda and salt in small mixer bowl. Add water, oil, vinegar and vanilla; beat 3 minutes on medium speed until thoroughly blended. Stir in SKOR Toffee Candy Bar pieces. Pour batter into paper-lined muffin cups (2½ inches in diameter), filling ⅔ full. Bake at 350° for 20 to 25 minutes or until cake tester inserted in center comes out clean. Cool; frost with Las Vegas Frosting. Garnish with additional SKOR Toffee Candy Bar pieces.

*Break SKOR candy into pieces; grind in food processor.

LAS VEGAS FROSTING

- 1 cup confectioners' sugar
- 3 tablespoons HERSHEY'S Cocoa
- 3 tablespoons butter or margarine, softened
- 2 tablespoons milk
- ½ teaspoon vanilla
- 1 SKOR Toffee Candy Bar (1.25 ounces), chopped*

Combine confectioners' sugar and HERSHEY'S Cocoa in small bowl. Cream butter or margarine and ½ cup of cocoa mixture in small mixer bowl. Add remaining cocoa mixture, milk and vanilla; beat to spreading consistency. Stir in chopped SKOR Toffee Candy Bar until blended.

*Break SKOR candy into pieces; grind in food processor.

BLACK AND WHITE CHEESEPIES*

Yield: 6 servings

- 2 tablespoons HERSHEY'S Cocoa
- 1 tablespoon milk
- ⅔ cup sweetened condensed milk, divided
- ½ teaspoon vanilla
- ¼ cup heavy or whipping cream
- 2 packages (3 ounces each), cream cheese, softened
- 1 tablespoon lemon juice
- 1 teaspoon vanilla
- Six (4-ounce package) miniature graham cracker tart shells

Combine HERSHEY'S Cocoa, milk and ⅓ cup of the sweetened condensed milk in small saucepan. Cook over low heat, stirring constantly, until mixture boils. Remove from heat; stir in ½ teaspoon vanilla. Cool completely.

Whip heavy cream until stiff; fold into chocolate mixture. Beat cream cheese in small mixer bowl until light and fluffy. Gradually beat in remaining condensed milk, the lemon juice and 1 teaspoon vanilla. Alternately spoon chocolate mixture and cheese mixture into tart shells, ending with chocolate. Cover; chill until firm.

BLACK AND WHITE COCONUT PIES*

Yield: 4 servings

Chocolate Crumb Crusts (below)
⅓ cup sugar
3 tablespoons cornstarch
1½ cups milk
2 egg yolks, beaten
1½ teaspoons butter
1 teaspoon vanilla
¼ cup flaked coconut
2 tablespoons HERSHEY'S Cocoa
2 tablespoons sugar
1 tablespoon milk
Sweetened whipped cream

Prepare Chocolate Crumb Crusts; set aside. Combine ⅓ cup sugar, the cornstarch, and 1½ cups milk in small saucepan. Blend in egg yolks. Cook over medium heat, stirring constantly, until mixture boils; boil and stir 1 minute. Remove from heat; stir in butter and vanilla. Pour ⅔ cup cooked mixture into small bowl; stir in coconut. Set aside.

Combine HERSHEY'S Cocoa, 2 tablespoons sugar and 1 tablespoon milk in small bowl; blend into remaining cooked mixture in saucepan. Cook over medium heat, stirring constantly, until mixture begins to boil; remove from heat.

Divide coconut mixture into prepared crumb crusts; top with chocolate mixture, spreading evenly. Press plastic wrap onto surfaces. Cool slightly; chill thoroughly. Top with sweetened whipped cream.

CHOCOLATE CRUMB CRUSTS

Combine ⅔ cup graham cracker crumbs, 2 tablespoons HERSHEY'S Cocoa and 2 tablespoons sugar in small bowl. Blend in 2 tablespoons melted butter. Press mixture firmly onto bottom and up sides of 4 miniature tart pans; chill.

FAST CHOCOLATE PECAN FUDGE*

Yield: about 2½ dozen pieces

¼ cup butter
6 tablespoons HERSHEY'S Cocoa
2 cups confectioners' sugar
½ teaspoon vanilla
¼ cup evaporated milk
¾ cup coarsely chopped pecans
Pecan halves, optional

Microwave butter in 1-quart micro-proof bowl on high (full power) for 30 seconds to 1 minute or until melted. Add HERSHEY'S Cocoa; stir until smooth. Stir in confectioners' sugar and vanilla; blend well (mixture will be dry and crumbly). Stir in evaporated milk; microwave on high for 30 seconds to 1 minute or until mixture is hot. Stir mixture until smooth; add coarsely chopped pecans. Pour mixture into aluminum foil-lined 8½ x 4½ x 2⅝-inch loaf pan. Garnish with pecan halves, if desired. Cover; chill until firm, about 2 hours. Cut into 1-inch squares. Store, covered, in refrigerator.

SPECIAL DARK TARTS*

Yield: 4 servings

1 HERSHEY'S SPECIAL DARK
  Sweet Chocolate Bar
  (4 ounces)
3 tablespoons milk
⅔ cup miniature marshmallows
⅓ cup heavy or whipping cream
4 miniature graham cracker tart
  shells
  Sweetened whipped cream
  Chocolate curls

Break HERSHEY'S SPECIAL DARK Sweet Chocolate Bar into pieces; combine with milk in top of double boiler over hot water. Stir until chocolate is melted and mixture is smooth. Add marshmallows; stir until smooth. Cool completely. Whip heavy cream until stiff; fold into chocolate mixture. Divide evenly among tart shells. Cover; chill until firm. Garnish with sweetened whipped cream and chocolate curls.

CLASSIC CHOCOLATE SAUCE

Yield: about ¾ cup sauce

1 block (1 ounce) HERSHEY'S
  Unsweetened Baking
  Chocolate
1 tablespoon butter
½ cup sugar
⅛ teaspoon salt
6 tablespoons evaporated milk
¼ teaspoon vanilla

Place HERSHEY'S Unsweetened Baking Chocolate and butter in small micro-proof bowl. Microwave on high (full power) for 30 seconds to 1 minute or until chocolate is softened and mixture is melted and smooth when stirred. Add sugar, salt and evaporated milk; blend well. Microwave on high for 1 to 2 minutes, stirring with wire whisk after each minute, or until mixture is smooth and hot; stir in vanilla. Serve warm over ice cream or other desserts.

RICH COCOA WAFFLES

Yield: about 5 four-inch waffles

½ cup unsifted all-purpose flour
6 tablespoons sugar
¼ cup HERSHEY'S Cocoa
¼ teaspoon baking powder
¼ teaspoon baking soda
⅛ teaspoon salt
½ cup buttermilk or sour milk*
1 egg
2 tablespoons butter or margarine,
  melted
  Ice cream
  Fresh fruit

Combine flour, sugar, HERSHEY'S Cocoa, baking powder, baking soda and salt in medium mixing bowl. Add buttermilk or sour milk and egg; beat just until blended. Gradually add melted butter or margarine, beating until smooth. Bake in waffle iron according to manufacturer's directions. Serve warm with ice cream and fresh fruit.

*To sour milk: Use 1½ teaspoons vinegar plus milk to equal ½ cup.

RUM HOT FUDGE PUDDING

Yield: 3 or 4 servings

½ cup unsifted all-purpose flour
6 tablespoons sugar
1½ tablespoons HERSHEY'S Cocoa
1 teaspoon baking powder
¼ cup milk
1 tablespoon vegetable oil
½ teaspoon vanilla
⅓ cup chopped nuts
6 tablespoons packed light brown sugar
2 tablespoons HERSHEY'S Cocoa
½ cup boiling water
2 tablespoons light *or* dark rum
Rum Whipped Cream (below)

Combine flour, 6 tablespoons sugar, 1½ tablespoons HERSHEY'S Cocoa and the baking powder in medium mixing bowl. Stir in milk, oil, vanilla and half of chopped nuts. Spread batter in 1½-quart micro-proof casserole or baking dish. Combine brown sugar, 2 tablespoons HERSHEY'S Cocoa, the remaining chopped nuts, boiling water and rum in small mixing bowl. Pour over batter in dish; *DO NOT MIX.* Cover with sheet of wax paper. Microwave on high (full power) for 4 to 6 minutes, rotating ¼ turn halfway through cooking time, or until cake rises to surface and sauce forms on bottom. Let stand 10 minutes before serving. Serve warm or cold topped with Rum Whipped Cream or ice cream.

RUM WHIPPED CREAM

Combine 1 cup heavy or whipping cream, 2 tablespoons confectioners' sugar and 1 tablespoon rum in small bowl; beat until stiff peaks form.

CHOCOLATE RUM BALLS

Yield: about 2 dozen balls

1⅔ cups crushed vanilla wafer cookies
6 tablespoons confectioners' sugar
¾ cup chopped nuts
2 tablespoons HERSHEY'S Cocoa
1½ tablespoons light corn syrup
¼ cup rum
Confectioners' sugar

Combine crushed vanilla wafers, 6 tablespoons confectioners' sugar, the nuts and HERSHEY'S Cocoa in medium mixing bowl. Blend in corn syrup and rum. Shape into 1-inch balls; roll in confectioners' sugar. Store in airtight container 3 to 4 days to develop flavor. Roll in additional confectioners' sugar before serving.

Special Dark Tarts, page 49.

BLACK AND WHITE CUPCAKES

Yield: about 1 dozen cupcakes

Cream Cheese Filling (below)
⅔ cup unsifted all-purpose flour
½ cup sugar
3 tablespoons HERSHEY'S Cocoa
¼ teaspoon baking soda
¼ teaspoon salt
½ cup buttermilk *or* sour milk*
3 tablespoons vegetable oil
1½ tablespoons beaten egg
½ teaspoon vanilla

Prepare Cream Cheese Filling; set aside. Combine flour, sugar, HERSHEY'S Cocoa, baking soda and salt in small mixer bowl. Add buttermilk or sour milk, oil, egg and vanilla; blend well. Fill paper-lined muffin cups (2½ inches in diameter) half full with batter. Spoon about 1 tablespoon Cream Cheese Filling onto each cupcake. Bake at 350° for 20 to 25 minutes or until cake tester inserted in cake portion comes out clean. Cool completely.

*To sour milk: Use 1½ teaspoons vinegar plus milk to equal ½ cup.

CREAM CHEESE FILLING

4 ounces cream cheese, softened
2½ tablespoons sugar
1½ tablespoons beaten egg
⅓ cup HERSHEY'S MINI CHIPS
    Semi-Sweet Chocolate

Blend cream cheese and sugar in small mixing bowl. Add egg; beat well. Stir in HERSHEY'S MINI CHIPS Semi-Sweet Chocolate.

INDIVIDUAL CHOCOLATE SOUFFLÉS

Yield: 4 servings

¼ cup butter *or* margarine,
    softened
⅔ cup sugar
½ teaspoon vanilla
2 eggs
⅓ cup unsifted all-purpose flour
⅓ cup HERSHEY'S Cocoa
¾ teaspoon baking powder
⅓ cup milk
½ cup heavy or whipping cream
1 tablespoon confectioners' sugar

Grease and sugar four 5 or 6-ounce ramekins or custard cups; set aside. Cream butter or margarine, sugar and vanilla in small mixer bowl until light and fluffy. Add eggs, one at a time, beating well after each addition. Combine flour, HERSHEY'S Cocoa and baking powder; add alternately with milk to creamed mixture. Beat 1 minute on medium speed. Divide batter evenly among prepared baking dishes. Place in 8-inch square pan; pour hot water into pans to depth of ½ inch around cups. Bake at 325° for 45 to 50 minutes or until cake tester inserted halfway between edge and center comes out clean. Remove from oven and allow to stand in water 5 minutes. Remove from water; cool slightly. Serve in baking dishes or invert into individual dessert dishes. Beat cream with confectioners' sugar until stiff; spoon onto warm soufflés.

CHOCOLATE INTIMATES

BAKED ALASKAS FOR TWO

Yield: 2 servings

½ cup shortening
1 cup sugar
1 teaspoon vanilla
1 egg
1 egg yolk
2 tablespoons milk
1 cup unsifted all-purpose flour
⅓ cup HERSHEY'S Cocoa
½ teaspoon baking powder
¼ teaspoon salt
  Meringue (below)
2 scoops mint-chocolate chip ice cream

Cream shortening, sugar and vanilla in small mixer bowl until light and fluffy. Add egg, egg yolk and milk; blend well. Combine flour, HERSHEY'S Cocoa, baking powder and salt; add to creamed mixture and blend well. Spread batter evenly in greased 9-inch square pan. Bake at 350° for 25 to 30 minutes or until brownie pulls away from pan edges. Cool in pan. Cut into 9 squares. To make two Baked Alaskas, place two brownie squares on ungreased cookie sheet. Prepare Meringue. Place scoop of ice cream in center of each brownie; cover ice cream and brownie completely with Meringue. Bake at 450° for 4 to 5 minutes or just until Meringue is lightly browned. Serve immediately. (To make additional servings: Prepare additional Meringue and assemble and bake as directed.) Freeze remaining brownies for later use.

MERINGUE

Beat 1 egg white and ⅛ teaspoon cream of tartar in small mixer bowl until foamy; gradually add 2 tablespoons sugar and continue beating at high speed until stiff peaks form.

LOVER'S MOUSSE FOR TWO*

Yield: 2 servings

2 tablespoons sugar
½ teaspoon unflavored gelatine
¼ cup milk
½ cup HERSHEY'S MINI CHIPS Semi-Sweet Chocolate
1 tablespoon orange-flavored liqueur or 1 teaspoon vanilla
½ cup heavy or whipping cream
  Sweetened whipped cream

Combine sugar and gelatine in small saucepan; stir in milk. Let stand several minutes to soften. Cook over medium heat, stirring constantly, just until mixture begins to boil. Remove from heat; immediately add HERSHEY'S MINI CHIPS Semi-Sweet Chocolate, stirring until melted. Blend in liqueur or vanilla; cool to room temperature. Beat heavy cream until stiff; gradually add chocolate mixture to cream, folding gently just until combined. Chill thoroughly; garnish with sweetened whipped cream before serving.

MERINGUE HEARTS WITH CHOCOLATE MOUSSE FILLING

Yield: 2 heart-shaped meringues

1 egg white
⅛ teaspoon cream of tartar
¼ cup sugar
Chocolate ribbons and candied cherry pieces

Cover a cookie sheet with brown paper or parchment paper. Draw 2 heart shapes, each about 4 inches across at the widest point, on the paper; set aside. Beat egg white and cream of tartar in small mixer bowl until foamy. Gradually beat in sugar, 1 tablespoon at a time; continue beating until glossy and very stiff peaks form. Spread meringue over heart shapes, building up sides. Bake in preheated oven at 275° for 45 minutes. Without opening door, turn off oven; let meringues remain in oven for 1½ hours. Remove from oven; cool completely. Wrap each tightly if made ahead. Prepare Chocolate Mousse Filling; spoon into meringues. Garnish with chocolate ribbons and candied cherry pieces.

CHOCOLATE MOUSSE FILLING

½ teaspoon unflavored gelatine
2 tablespoons cold water
¼ cup sugar
2 tablespoons HERSHEY'S Cocoa
½ cup heavy or whipping cream, very cold
½ teaspoon vanilla

Sprinkle gelatine onto water in custard cup; stir and let stand 1 minute. Place custard cup in small pan with hot water; stir until gelatine is completely dissolved. Remove from water bath; cool. Combine sugar and HERSHEY'S Cocoa in small mixer bowl, blending well. Add heavy cream and vanilla. Beat at medium speed until stiff peaks form; pour in gelatine mixture and beat until well blended. Chill slightly.

RUM HOT CHOCOLATE

Yield: 3 servings (6 ounces each)

¼ cup sugar
2 tablespoons HERSHEY'S Cocoa
3 tablespoons water
2 cups milk
2 tablespoons light *or* dark rum
Sweetened whipped cream
Cinnamon sticks

Combine sugar and HERSHEY'S Cocoa in small saucepan; blend in water. Cook over medium heat, stirring constantly, until mixture boils; boil and stir 2 minutes. Add milk; heat to serving temperature, stirring occasionally (do not boil). Remove from heat; add rum. Serve hot, garnished with sweetened whipped cream and cinnamon sticks.

Meringue Hearts with Chocolate Mousse Filling, this page.

DOUBLE CHOCOLATE COOLER

Yield: 2 servings (10 ounces each)

1 cup club soda, chilled
1 cup chocolate ice cream
3 tablespoons HERSHEY'S Chocolate Flavored Syrup
3 tablespoons heavy or whipping cream

Combine all ingredients in blender container; blend until smooth. Serve immediately.

CHOCOLATE TWIST

Yield: 2 servings (5 ounces each)

1 cup half-and-half
3 tablespoons HERSHEY'S Chocolate Flavored Syrup
3 tablespoons orange-flavored liqueur

Measure all ingredients into pitcher; stir until well blended. Serve over crushed ice.

QUICK COCOA DRINK

Yield: one 8-ounce serving

1 tablespoon sugar
2 teaspoons HERSHEY'S Cocoa
1 tablespoon very hot tap water
1 cup cold milk
¼ teaspoon vanilla, optional

Combine sugar and HERSHEY'S Cocoa in tall glass; blend well. Add hot water; stir until sugar is dissolved and mixture is well blended. Stir in cold milk and vanilla, if desired; stir until blended.

EASY COCOA PUDDING*

Yield: 2 or 3 servings

2 tablespoons cold milk
1 teaspoon unflavored gelatine
⅓ cup very hot milk
6 tablespoons sugar
2 tablespoons HERSHEY'S Cocoa
½ teaspoon vanilla
¼ cup heavy or whipping cream
⅓ cup crushed ice
Sweetened whipped cream
1 Banana, sliced

Pour cold milk into blender container. Sprinkle gelatine onto cold milk; let stand several minutes to soften. Add hot milk; blend 2 minutes on low speed or until gelatine is completely dissolved. Add sugar, HERSHEY'S Cocoa and vanilla; blend well. Add heavy cream and crushed ice; continue processing until ice is liquefied. Allow to stand several minutes to thicken slightly. Pour into bowl or individual dessert dishes. Cover; chill at least 20 minutes or until set. Garnish with sweetened whipped cream and banana slices before serving.

CHOCOLATE CREME DE BANANA DRINK

Yield: 2 servings (7 ounces each)

½ cup half-and-half
¼ cup mashed ripe banana
¼ cup banana-flavored liqueur
3 tablespoons HERSHEY'S
   Chocolate Flavored Syrup
1¼ cups ice cubes

Measure all ingredients into blender container. Cover; blend on high speed for 2 minutes. Decrease speed; blend 1 minute longer or until frothy. Serve immediately.

CHOCOLATE CREME DE MENTHE DRINK

Yield: 2 servings (6 ounces each)

1 cup half-and-half
3 tablespoons HERSHEY'S
   Chocolate Flavored Syrup
2 tablespoons white creme de
   menthe liqueur

Measure all ingredients into pitcher; stir until well blended. Serve over crushed ice.

CHOCOLATE RUSSIAN

Yield: 2 servings (6 ounces each)

1¼ cups half-and-half
3 tablespoons HERSHEY'S
   Chocolate Flavored Syrup
2 tablespoons vodka
1½ tablespoons coffee-flavored
   liqueur

Measure ingredients into small pitcher; stir until well blended. Serve over crushed ice.

MINTY HOT CHOCOLATE

Yield: 3 servings (7 ounces each)

¼ cup sugar
3 tablespoons HERSHEY'S Cocoa
½ cup water
2 cups milk
2 tablespoons creme de menthe
   liqueur
½ cup heavy or whipping cream
1 tablespoon confectioners' sugar
1 tablespoon crushed hard
   peppermint candy

Combine sugar and HERSHEY'S Cocoa in small saucepan; stir in water. Cook over medium heat, stirring constantly, until mixture boils; boil and stir 2 minutes. Add milk; heat thoroughly (do not boil). Add liqueur. Beat with rotary beater until smooth and foamy; pour into cups. Whip heavy cream and confectioners' sugar until stiff; fold in crushed peppermint candy. Top each drink with a heaping spoonful of whipped cream mixture. Serve immediately.

PEARS AU CHOCOLAT*

Yield: 2 servings

2 fresh pears
¼ cup sugar
½ cup water
½ teaspoon vanilla
  Nut filling, optional (below)
  Creamy Chocolate Sauce
  (below)

Core pears from bottom end but leave stems intact; peel. Slice small amount from bottom of each pear to make a flat base. Combine sugar and water in small saucepan; add pears. Cover; simmer over low heat 15 to 20 minutes (depending on ripeness of pears). Remove from heat; add vanilla. Cool pears in syrup; chill. At serving time, drain pears; spoon in Nut Filling, if desired. Place in serving dish. Prepare Creamy Chocolate Sauce; spoon sauce onto each pear. Serve with remaining sauce.

NUT FILLING

Combine 3 tablespoons finely chopped nuts, 1 tablespoon confectioners' sugar and ½ teaspoon milk in small bowl until mixture holds together.

CREAMY CHOCOLATE SAUCE

3 tablespoons water
3 tablespoons sugar
2 tablespoons butter
⅔ cup HERSHEY'S MINI CHIPS
  Semi-Sweet Chocolate

Combine water, sugar and butter in small saucepan; cook over medium heat, stirring constantly, until mixture comes to full boil. Remove from heat; stir in HERSHEY'S MINI CHIPS Semi-Sweet Chocolate. Stir until chocolate has completely melted; beat or whisk until smooth. Cool.

FROZEN MOUSSE FOR TWO*

Yield: 2 servings

1 HERSHEY'S Milk Chocolate Bar
  (4 ounces)
2 tablespoons water
1 egg, beaten
½ cup heavy or whipping cream

Break HERSHEY'S Milk Chocolate Bar into pieces; combine with water in medium micro-proof bowl. Microwave on high (full power) for 30 seconds to 1 minute or until mixture is melted and smooth when stirred. Stir in beaten egg. Microwave on medium (½ power) for 30 seconds to 1 minute or until mixture is hot, but not boiling. Cool slightly. Whip heavy cream until stiff; fold into cooled chocolate mixture. Pour into 2 dessert dishes. Cover; freeze until firm.

Pears Au Chocolat, this page.

INDIVIDUAL CHOCOLATE CHEESECAKES*

Yield: 2 servings

Graham Crumb Shells (below)
1 package (3 ounces) cream cheese, softened
2 tablespoons sugar
⅓ cup HERSHEY'S MINI CHIPS Semi-Sweet Chocolate
1 egg
½ teaspoon vanilla
Sweetened whipped cream
Fresh fruit

Prepare Graham Crumb Shells; set aside. Beat cream cheese and sugar in small mixer bowl. Place HERSHEY'S MINI CHIPS Semi-Sweet Chocolate in small bowl; melt by setting in pan of hot water or melt in microwave. Stir until completely melted; add to cream cheese mixture. Beat in egg and vanilla until well blended. Spoon into prepared shells, filling cups ¾ full; bake at 350° for 20 to 25 minutes or until set. Cool completely; chill. Garnish with sweetened whipped cream and fresh fruit before serving.

GRAHAM CRUMB SHELLS

Combine ¼ cup graham cracker crumbs, 2 teaspoons sugar and 1 tablespoon melted butter in small bowl; press mixture onto bottom and ½ inch up sides of 4 paper-lined muffin cups (2½ inches in diameter) or two 6-ounce custard cups or small ramekins.

MOUSSE IN CHOCOLATE CUPS*

Yield: 2 servings

½ cup HERSHEY'S MINI CHIPS Semi-Sweet Chocolate
Chocolate Mousse (below)

Melt HERSHEY'S MINI CHIPS Semi-Sweet Chocolate in microwave on high (full power) for 1 to 1½ minutes or in top of double boiler over hot water. With soft pastry brush, coat inside pleated surface and bottom of 2 paper-lined muffin cups (2½ inches in diameter) with melted chocolate. Chill 10 minutes; coat thin spots. Chill thoroughly. Remove from refrigerator; gently peel off paper. Cover; store in refrigerator. Prepare Chocolate Mousse; spoon into Chocolate Cups. Cover; chill until set.

CHOCOLATE MOUSSE

½ teaspoon unflavored gelatine
1½ teaspoons cold water
1 tablespoon boiling water
¼ cup sugar
2 tablespoons HERSHEY'S Cocoa
½ cup heavy or whipping cream, very cold
½ teaspoon vanilla

Sprinkle gelatine onto cold water in small bowl; let stand several minutes to soften. Add boiling water; stir until gelatine is completely dissolved (mixture must be clear). Stir together sugar and HERSHEY'S Cocoa in small, cold mixer bowl; add heavy cream and vanilla. Beat at medium speed until stiff peaks form; spoon into gelatine mixture and beat until well blended.

CHOCOLATE INTERNATIONALE

MADELEINES AU CHOCOLAT

Yield: about 1½ dozen filled cookies

1¼ cups unsifted all-purpose flour
1 cup sugar
¾ cup butter, melted
5 tablespoons HERSHEY'S Cocoa
3 eggs
2 egg yolks
½ teaspoon vanilla
Chocolate Frosting (below)

Lightly grease the indentations of a madeleine mold pan (each shell is 3 x 2 inches); set aside. Combine flour and sugar in medium saucepan. Combine melted butter and HERSHEY'S Cocoa; stir into the dry ingredients. With a fork, lightly beat eggs, egg yolks and vanilla in small bowl until well blended; stir into chocolate mixture, blending well. Cook over very low heat, stirring constantly, until mixture is warm; do not simmer or boil. Remove from heat. Fill each mold half full with batter. Bake at 350° for 8 to 10 minutes or until cake tester comes out clean. Invert onto wire rack; cool completely. Frost flat sides of cookies with Chocolate Frosting. Press frosted sides together, forming shells.

CHOCOLATE FROSTING

2½ cups confectioners' sugar
¼ cup HERSHEY'S Cocoa
¼ cup butter, softened
4 to 5 tablespoons milk
1 teaspoon vanilla

Combine confectioners' sugar and HERSHEY'S Cocoa in small mixing bowl. Cream butter and ½ cup of the confectioners' sugar-cocoa mixture in small mixer bowl until light and fluffy. Alternately add remaining cocoa mixture with milk; beat to spreading consistency. Stir in vanilla.

BLENDER POTS DE CREME*

Yield: 4 servings

1 egg
⅓ cup sugar
¼ cup HERSHEY'S Cocoa
¼ cup butter, softened
¼ teaspoon vanilla
⅓ cup hot milk
Sweetened whipped cream

Combine egg, sugar, HERSHEY'S Cocoa, butter and vanilla in blender container; blend until smooth, scraping sides of container frequently. Add hot milk; blend on high speed until smooth, scraping sides of container occasionally. Pour into 4 pots de creme containers or demitasse cups; press plastic wrap directly onto surface. Chill several hours or until set. Garnish with sweetened whipped cream.

BLACK FOREST TORTE*

Yield: 4 to 6 servings

Cherry Filling (below)
1 cup unsifted all-purpose flour
1 cup sugar
6 tablespoons HERSHEY'S Cocoa
1 teaspoon baking soda
½ teaspoon baking powder
1 egg
½ cup strong black coffee
½ cup buttermilk *or* sour milk*
¼ cup vegetable oil
½ teaspoon vanilla
Kirsch Whipped Cream (below)

Prepare Cherry Filling. Chill several hours.

Grease 9-inch square pan. Line with wax paper and grease paper; dust with flour. Combine flour, sugar, HERSHEY'S Cocoa, baking soda and baking powder in small mixer bowl. Add egg, coffee, buttermilk, oil and vanilla. Beat on medium speed 2 minutes (batter will be thin). Pour batter into prepared pan. Bake at 350° for 30 to 35 minutes or until cake tester inserted in center comes out clean. Cool 10 minutes; remove from pan and remove wax paper. Cool completely. Cut cake into two equal rectangles.

Prepare Kirsch Whipped Cream. Place 1 cake layer upside down on serving plate. With decorator's tube or spoon, make ring of frosting ½ inch high and 1 inch wide around edge of layer. Fill center with about 1 cup Cherry Filling. Carefully place second layer top side up on filling. Alternate remaining filling and piped frosting in diagonal stripes across top layer of cake. Chill at least 1 hour before serving.

*To sour milk: Use 1½ teaspoons vinegar plus milk to equal ½ cup.

CHERRY FILLING

Combine 2 cups canned cherry pie filling and 1⅓ tablespoons each of sugar and Kirsch. Chill several hours.

KIRSCH WHIPPED CREAM

Beat 1 cup heavy or whipping cream with 3 tablespoons confectioners' sugar and 1 teaspoon Kirsch until stiff.

Black Forest Torte, this page.

REGAL CHOCOLATE TORTE*

Yield: 6 servings

⅓ cup butter *or* margarine
2 tablespoons vegetable oil
6 tablespoons HERSHEY'S Cocoa
1 cup sugar
2 eggs
2 tablespoons almond-flavored liqueur
1 cup unsifted all-purpose flour
¼ teaspoon baking powder
¼ teaspoon salt
½ cup chopped almonds
Chocolate Ganache Glaze (below)
Chocolate Whipped Cream (below)
Chocolate Triangles (next page)

Lightly grease 8¼-inch round micro-proof baking dish; line with parchment paper and set aside. Place butter or margarine and oil in medium micro-proof mixing bowl; microwave on high (full power) about 1 minute or until melted. Stir in cocoa, blending until smooth; blend in sugar. Add eggs and liqueur; beat well. Stir in flour, baking powder, salt and nuts. Spread batter into prepared baking dish. Microwave on medium (½ power) for 7 minutes, turning ¼ turn every 3 minutes of cooking time. Microwave on high (full power) for 1½ to 2½ minutes or until brownies begin to puff on top. (Do not microwave until completely dry on top; 1-inch wet spot will remain in center.) Cover with aluminum foil and let stand until completely cool. Run knife around edge of dish to loosen brownie; invert onto serving plate. Cover; chill thoroughly. Spread Chocolate Ganache Glaze on top and sides of chilled torte; refrigerate until glaze hardens. Garnish with Chocolate Whipped Cream and Chocolate Triangles. Serve chilled, cut into wedges.

CHOCOLATE GANACHE GLAZE

Break 4 blocks (4 ounces) HERSHEY'S Semi-Sweet Baking Chocolate into small pieces. Combine chocolate pieces and ¼ cup heavy cream in small micro-proof bowl. Microwave on high (full power) for 30 seconds to 1 minute or just until chocolate is melted and mixture is smooth when stirred. Cool slightly, just until thickened.

CHOCOLATE WHIPPED CREAM

1 cup heavy or whipping cream
2 tablespoons confectioners' sugar
1 tablespoon HERSHEY'S Cocoa
½ teaspoon vanilla

Combine cream, confectioners' sugar, HERSHEY'S Cocoa and vanilla in small mixer bowl; beat until stiff peaks form.

CHOCOLATE TRIANGLES

Melt ⅔ cup HERSHEY'S MINI CHIPS Semi-Sweet Chocolate in top of double boiler over hot, not boiling, water; stir until completely melted. (Or melt in microwave oven.) With spatula, spread melted chocolate into 7-inch square on wax paper-covered cookie sheet. Chill 5 to 8 minutes or just until chocolate begins to set.

With sharp knife, cut chocolate square into smaller squares; cut each small square diagonally in half to make triangles. Do not try to separate at this time; chill until very firm. Carefully peel wax paper away from chocolate; separate triangles. Cover and refrigerate until ready to use.

ITALIAN DESSERT PUFFS

Yield: 6 servings

Six (10-ounce package) frozen patty shells
¾ cup ricotta cheese
2 tablespoons sugar
1 teaspoon grated orange rind
2 tablespoons chopped maraschino cherries
½ cup heavy or whipping cream
½ cup HERSHEY'S MINI CHIPS Semi-Sweet Chocolate

Bake patty shells according to package directions; cool. Beat ricotta cheese and sugar until smooth; blend in orange rind and cherries. Whip cream until stiff into small mixer bowl; fold in ricotta mixture and HERSHEY'S MINI CHIPS Semi-Sweet Chocolate. Spoon mixture into patty shells. Serve cold.

CROISSANTS WITH CHOCOLATE SAUCE

Yield: 4 servings

Chocolate Sauce (below)
4 frozen, ready prepared croissants, thawed and split lengthwise
1 cup cherry, peach or apple pie filling
Sweetened whipped cream

Prepare Chocolate Sauce; set aside. Heat croissants; cool. To serve, spoon generous amount of pie filling onto each croissant bottom. Replace tops and spoon on dollop of sweetened whipped cream and Chocolate Sauce.

CHOCOLATE SAUCE

3 tablespoons HERSHEY'S Cocoa
½ cup sugar
⅓ cup evaporated milk
2 tablespoons butter
¼ teaspoon vanilla

Combine HERSHEY'S Cocoa and sugar in small saucepan; stir in milk. Add butter; cook over low heat, stirring constantly, until mixture boils. Remove from heat; stir in butter and vanilla. Cool slightly; serve warm.

STRAWBERRY & CHOCOLATE MOUSSE*

Yield: 4 servings

- **1 package (10 ounces) frozen strawberries, thawed**
- **1 envelope unflavored gelatine**
- **¼ cup cold water**
- **½ cup milk**
- **⅓ cup HERSHEY'S Cocoa**
- **¼ cup sugar**
- **½ teaspoon vanilla**
- **1 cup heavy or whipping cream**
  Fresh strawberries
  Chocolate leaves

Drain strawberries, reserving 3 tablespoons of the syrup; set aside. Sprinkle gelatine onto water in blender container; let stand 5 minutes to soften. Meanwhile, heat milk in small saucepan over low heat until hot; do not boil. Add hot milk to gelatine mixture; blend on medium speed until gelatine is dissolved. Add HERSHEY'S Cocoa and sugar; blend on medium speed until sugar is dissolved. Add strawberries, reserved strawberry syrup and vanilla; blend well. Add heavy cream; blend well. Pour into 4 dessert dishes. Cover; chill several hours or overnight. Garnish with fresh strawberries and chocolate leaves.

COCOA CREME DE MENTHE PUNCH*

Yield: 4 servings (6 ounces each)

- **½ cup sugar**
- **¼ cup HERSHEY'S Cocoa**
- **2 cups milk**
- **½ cup heavy or whipping cream**
- **3 eggs, beaten**
- **¼ cup creme de cacao liqueur**
- **¼ cup white creme de menthe liqueur**

Combine sugar, HERSHEY'S Cocoa and ½ cup of the milk in small saucepan. Cook over medium heat, stirring constantly, until sugar is dissolved and mixture is smooth. Remove from heat; add remaining 1½ cups milk, the cream, eggs and liqueurs. Chill thoroughly. Beat with rotary beater just before serving. Serve in cups over crushed ice.

HURRY-UP HOT COCOA

Yield: One 6-ounce serving

- **2 tablespoons sugar**
- **1 tablespoon HERSHEY'S Cocoa**
  Dash salt
- **¾ cup very hot milk**
- **⅛ teaspoon vanilla, optional**

Combine sugar, HERSHEY'S Cocoa and salt in cup; stir in hot milk to fill cup. Add vanilla, if desired; stir until blended.

VARIATIONS:

Canadian Cocoa: Add ⅛ teaspoon maple extract.

Irish Mint Cocoa: Add ⅛ teaspoon pure mint or peppermint extract.

Orange Cocoa Cappuccino: Add ⅛ teaspoon pure orange extract.

Swiss Mocha: Add ½ teaspoon instant coffee granules.

Strawberry & Chocolate Mousse, this page.

CHOCOLATE ITALIAN CASSATA CAKE

Yield: 4 to 6 servings

1 package (16 ounces) golden pound cake mix with vegetable shortening *or* **frozen poundcake**
2 tablespoons anisette liqueur
1 cup ricotta cheese
¼ cup sugar
½ cup HERSHEY'S MINI CHIPS Semi-Sweet Chocolate
Chocolate Glaze (below)

Prepare pound cake mix according to package directions, baking in two loaf pans (8½ x 4½ x 2⅝ inches); bake as directed. Cool completely. Wrap and freeze one cake for later use. Trim cake so top is flat. Cut cake into 3 equal layers. Combine ricotta, sugar and HERSHEY'S MINI CHIPS Semi-Sweet Chocolate. Sprinkle bottom layer with 1 tablespoon liqueur; spread half of filling over layers. Repeat with middle layer and remaining filling and liqueur. Place remaining layer on top; glaze with Chocolate Glaze.

CHOCOLATE GLAZE

Melt 1 tablespoon butter in small saucepan; add 2 tablespoons HERSHEY'S Cocoa and 1½ tablespoons water, stirring until smooth. Remove from heat. Blend in 1 cup confectioners' sugar and ½ teaspoon vanilla; beat until smooth.

GERMAN CHOCOLATE CAKE

Yield: 4 to 6 servings

½ cup flaked coconut
¼ cup chopped pecans
2½ tablespoons packed light brown sugar
1½ tablespoons butter, melted
1½ tablespoons evaporated milk
1 tablespoon light corn syrup
¼ cup butter, softened
⅔ cup sugar
1 egg
¼ teaspoon vanilla
¾ cup unsifted all-purpose flour
3 tablespoons HERSHEY'S Cocoa
½ teaspoon baking soda
½ cup buttermilk

Line 8-inch layer pan with foil; butter foil. Combine coconut, pecans, brown sugar, 1½ tablespoons melted butter, the evaporated milk and corn syrup in small bowl. Spread mixture evenly over bottom of prepared pan. Cream ¼ cup butter and the sugar in small mixer bowl until light and fluffy. Add egg and vanilla; blend well. Combine flour, HERSHEY'S Cocoa and baking soda; add alternately with buttermilk to creamed mixture. Carefully spread batter over coconut layer; do not mix with coconut topping. Bake at 350° for 30 to 35 minutes or until top springs back when touched. Invert immediately onto wire rack; gently remove foil and discard. Cover loosely with foil to keep topping soft. Cool completely. Keep well covered.

CHOCOLATE FROID

ICE CREAM WITH HERSHEY'S SYRUP*

Yield: about 1 quart ice cream

- 1 envelope unflavored gelatine
- ¼ cup cold water
- ½ cup milk
- 6 tablespoons sugar
- ¾ cup HERSHEY'S Chocolate Flavored Syrup
- 1 cup light cream
- 1 cup heavy or whipping cream
- 1 tablespoon vanilla

Sprinkle gelatine onto cold water in medium saucepan; let stand several minutes to soften. Add milk and sugar; cook over medium heat, stirring constantly, until gelatine and sugar are dissolved and mixture is warm. Remove from heat; add HERSHEY'S Chocolate Flavored Syrup. Cool 10 minutes; add light cream, heavy or whipping cream and vanilla. Freeze in miniature ice cream freezer (2-quart) according to manufacturer's directions.

CHOCOLATE LIQUEUR SAUCE

Yield: about 1 cup sauce

- 2 tablespoons butter
- 3 tablespoons HERSHEY'S Cocoa
- ½ cup sugar
- ⅛ teaspoon salt
- 6 tablespoons light cream
- 1½ teaspoons liqueur (creme de menthe, amaretto, or Grand Marnier)

Melt butter in small saucepan over low heat; remove from heat. Stir in HERSHEY'S Cocoa, sugar and salt. Add light cream and blend well. Cook over low heat, stirring constantly, until mixture just begins to boil. Remove from heat; stir in liqueur. Serve warm over ice cream or other desserts.

CHOCOLATE COVERED BANANAS

Yield: 4 servings

- 2 medium bananas
- 4 wooden skewers
- 1 cup HERSHEY'S MINI CHIPS Semi-Sweet Chocolate
- 1 tablespoon shortening (NOT butter, margarine or oil)
- ¾ cup coarsely chopped unsalted peanuts

Peel bananas; cut in half crosswise. Insert skewer into each banana piece; place on wax paper-covered tray. Cover; freeze until firm. Melt HERSHEY'S MINI CHIPS Semi-Sweet Chocolate and shortening in top of double boiler over hot water. Remove bananas from freezer just before dipping. Dip each piece into warm chocolate, covering completely. Allow excess to drip off; immediately roll in chopped peanuts. Cover; return to freezer. Serve frozen.

ICE CREAM SHELLS WITH FUDGE SAUCE*

Yield: 6 servings

Six (10-ounce package) frozen patty shells
2 cups (1 pint) favorite flavor ice cream
Fudge Sauce (below)
Chocolate curls, chocolate leaves *or* fresh fruit

Bake patty shells according to package directions; cool. Fill cooled shells with ice cream; freeze. Pour Fudge Sauce over shells before serving. Garnish with chocolate curls, chocolate leaves or fresh fruit.

FUDGE SAUCE

6 tablespoons sugar
¼ cup HERSHEY'S Cocoa
⅓ cup evaporated milk
2 tablespoons light corn syrup
2½ tablespoons butter
1 teaspoon vanilla

Combine sugar and HERSHEY'S Cocoa in small saucepan; blend in evaporated milk and corn syrup. Cook over medium heat, stirring constantly, until mixture boils; boil and stir 1 minute. Remove from heat; stir in butter and vanilla. Serve slightly warm.

COCOA-FRUIT SHERBET*

Yield: about 4 servings

½ medium-size ripe banana
¾ cup orange juice
½ cup half-and-half
¼ cup sugar
2 tablespoons HERSHEY'S Cocoa
1 teaspoon orange-flavored liqueur

Slice banana into blender container. Add orange juice; blend until smooth. Add remaining ingredients; blend well. Pour into 8½ x 4½ x 2⅝-inch loaf pan or ice cube tray; freeze until hard around edges. Spoon mixture into blender container or small mixer bowl; blend until smooth. Pour into 2-cup mold; freeze until firm. To serve, unmold onto chilled plate and slice.

CHOCOLATE NUT SAUCE

Yield: about 1 cup sauce

2½ tablespoons butter
⅓ cup coarsely chopped pecans *or* almonds
⅔ cup sugar
¼ cup HERSHEY'S Cocoa
⅛ teaspoon salt
½ cup light cream
½ teaspoon vanilla

Melt butter in small saucepan over low heat; sauté chopped nuts in melted butter until lightly browned. Remove from heat; stir in sugar, HERSHEY'S Cocoa and salt. Add light cream; blend well. Cook over low heat, stirring constantly, until mixture just begins to boil. Remove from heat; add vanilla. Serve warm over ice cream or other desserts.

Ice Cream Shells with Fudge Sauce, this page.

CHOCOLATE-MINT PARFAITS*

Yield: 2 parfaits

1 envelope dessert topping mix
6 tablespoons cold milk
1 teaspoon green creme de menthe liqueur
4 to 5 drops green food color
3 tablespoons HERSHEY'S Chocolate Flavored Syrup
1 teaspoon creme de cacao liqueur
Additional HERSHEY'S Chocolate Flavored Syrup

Combine topping mix and milk in small mixer bowl. Beat on high speed about 2 minutes or until soft peaks form; beat 2 minutes longer until mixture is light and fluffy. Transfer half of mixture to a small bowl; blend in creme de menthe and food color. To remaining mixture, add HERSHEY'S Chocolate Flavored Syrup and creme de cacao, beating to blend thoroughly. Alternately spoon mixtures into 2 parfait glasses. Place in freezer 3 to 4 hours. Garnish with additional HERSHEY'S Chocolate Flavored Syrup, if desired.

MOCHA ICE CREAM ROLL*

Yield: 6 servings

3 egg yolks, at room temperature
6 tablespoons sugar, divided
½ teaspoon vanilla
3 egg whites, at room temperature
2½ tablespoons HERSHEY'S Cocoa
1½ tablespoons flour
2 cups (1 pint) coffee ice cream
Fudge Mocha Sauce (next page)
Fruit, optional

Grease 13 x 9-inch pan; line with wax paper and lightly grease paper. Set aside. Beat egg yolks in small mixer bowl on high speed; gradually add 2 tablespoons of the sugar and the vanilla, beating until thick and lemon colored. Beat egg whites in separate small mixer bowl; gradually add 2 tablespoons of the sugar, beating until stiff but not dry. Carefully fold egg yolk mixture into beaten egg whites. Combine remaining 2 tablespoons sugar, the HERSHEY'S Cocoa and flour; fold about 2 tablespoons at a time into egg mixture just until blended.

Spread batter evenly in prepared pan. Bake at 375° for 10 to 12 minutes or just until cake springs back when touched lightly in center. Invert onto slightly dampened towel; carefully peel off wax paper. Immediately roll cake and towel together, starting from narrow end; place on wire rack to cool completely.

Carefully unroll cake; remove towel. Quickly spread with softened ice cream. Reroll; wrap and place in freezer. Freeze completely. At serving time, drizzle with Fudge Mocha Sauce; slice and serve with additional sauce and fruit, if desired.

FUDGE MOCHA SAUCE

6 tablespoons sugar
¼ cup HERSHEY'S Cocoa
⅓ cup evaporated milk
2 tablespoons light corn syrup
2½ tablespoons butter
1 teaspoon coffee-flavored liqueur

Combine sugar and HERSHEY'S Cocoa in small saucepan; blend in evaporated milk and corn syrup. Cook over medium heat, stirring constantly, until mixture boils; boil and stir 1 minute. Remove from heat; stir in butter and liqueur. Serve slightly warm.

TORTONI WITH A TWIST*

Yield: 6 servings

½ cup REESE'S Peanut Butter
   Chips
1 cup heavy or whipping cream
½ cup coconut cookie crumbs*
¼ cup confectioners' sugar
1 teaspoon rum
6 maraschino cherry halves,
   drained

Chop REESE'S Peanut Butter Chips in nut chopper or by hand. (Do not use blender or food processor.) Set aside.

Combine ½ cup heavy cream with the coconut cookie crumbs, confectioners' sugar and rum. Cover and chill 30 minutes. Beat remaining ½ cup heavy cream until stiff; fold in chilled cream-cookie crumb mixture and chopped peanut butter chips. Fill paper-lined muffin cups (2½ inches in diameter) with mixture. Cover; freeze until firm. Top with maraschino cherry halves just before serving.

*Any type hard coconut cookie may be used; use blender or food processor to make crumbs.

CHOCOLATE RUM-NUT ICE CREAM*

Yield: about 1 quart ice cream

1 cup sugar
2 tablespoons flour
1 cup milk
1 egg, slightly beaten
2 blocks (2 ounces) HERSHEY'S
   Unsweetened Baking
   Chocolate, broken into pieces
½ teaspoon rum extract
⅓ cup chopped nuts
1 tablespoon butter
2 cups (1 pint) light cream

Combine sugar and flour in medium saucepan; gradually stir in milk. Blend in beaten egg and HERSHEY'S Unsweetened Baking Chocolate pieces. Cook over medium heat, stirring constantly, until mixture boils; boil and stir 1 minute. Remove from heat; add rum extract. Blend with wire whisk until mixture is smooth. Chill thoroughly. Meanwhile, sauté nuts in butter over medium heat in small pan; cool. Add light cream to chilled mixture; blend well. Freeze in miniature ice cream freezer (2-quart) according to manufacturers' directions.

EASY CHOCOLATE FROZEN YOGURT*

Yield: about 1 pint

¼ cup HERSHEY'S Cocoa
¼ cup sugar
2 containers (8 ounces each)
    vanilla yogurt
¼ cup light corn syrup

Combine HERSHEY'S Cocoa and sugar in small bowl; set aside. Combine yogurt, corn syrup and cocoa mixture until well blended and smooth in medium mixing bowl; pour into foil-lined loaf pan (9¼ x 5¼ x 2¾ inches). Cover; freeze several hours or overnight until firm. Spoon into large mixer bowl. With mixer at low speed, beat until smooth but not melted. Return to loaf pan or pour into 1-pint freezer container. Cover; freeze until firm. Before serving, allow to stand several minutes at room temperature.

EASY CHOCOLATE ICE CREAM

Yield: about 4 servings

⅔ cup sweetened condensed
    milk (NOT evaporated)
½ cup HERSHEY'S Chocolate
    Flavored Syrup
1 cup heavy or whipping cream,
    whipped
    Additional HERSHEY'S
    Chocolate Flavored Syrup,
    optional

Combine sweetened condensed milk and ½ cup HERSHEY'S Chocolate Flavored Syrup in medium mixer bowl. Fold in whipped cream until blended. Pour into loaf pan (8½ x 4½ x 2⅝ inches). Cover; freeze until firm. Scoop into dessert dishes. Serve topped with additional HERSHEY'S Chocolate Flavored Syrup.

ICE CREAM WITH HERSHEY BAR

Yield: about 1½ quarts ice cream

2 tablespoons sugar
1 tablespoon flour
¼ teaspoon salt
½ cup light cream
1 egg, slightly beaten
1 HERSHEY'S Milk Chocolate Bar
    (8 ounces), broken into pieces
1 teaspoon vanilla
1½ cups light cream
½ cup heavy or whipping cream

Combine sugar, flour and salt in small saucepan; add ½ cup light cream. Cook over medium heat, stirring constantly, until mixture boils; boil and stir 1 minute. Remove from heat. Gradually stir small amount of cooked mixture into egg; blend well. Return egg mixture to cooked mixture in saucepan; stir until well blended. Add HERSHEY'S Milk Chocolate Bar pieces and vanilla; stir until melted. (If necessary, place over low heat until melted.)

Pour into large mixing bowl. Add 1½ cups light cream and the heavy cream; blend well. Chill. Freeze in ice cream freezer according to manufacturer's directions.

Mocha Ice Cream Roll, page 72.

SKOR CANDY BUTTER BRICKLE ICE CREAM*

Yield: 6 servings

3 egg yolks
1⅓ cups (14-ounce can) sweetened condensed milk (*NOT* evaporated)
3 tablespoons water
1 tablespoon vanilla
1¼ cups finely chopped SKOR Toffee Candy Bars (about five 1.25-ounce bars)
2 cups heavy or whipping cream

Beat egg yolks with wire whisk in large mixing bowl; stir in sweetened condensed milk, water and vanilla. Chop SKOR Toffee Candy Bars by hand or in food processor; set aside. Beat heavy cream in large mixer bowl until stiff; fold with chopped SKOR Bars into egg yolk mixture. Pour into aluminum foil-lined loaf pan (9¼ x 5¼ x 2¾ inches). Cover; freeze until firm.

HERSHEY 2 FOR 1 SAUCE

Yield: about ½ cup sauce

¼ cup HERSHEY'S Chocolate Fudge Topping
¼ cup HERSHEY'S Chocolate Flavored Syrup

Combine HERSHEY'S Chocolate Fudge Topping and HERSHEY'S Chocolate Flavored Syrup in small saucepan. Cook over low heat, stirring constantly, just until mixture is warm and well blended. Serve warm over ice cream or other desserts.

ALL-IN-ONE SUNDAE TOPPING

Yield: about ⅔ cup topping

3 HERSHEY'S MR. GOODBAR Chocolate Bars (1.65 ounces each), broken into pieces
3 large marshmallows
2 tablespoons milk

Combine HERSHEY'S MR. GOODBAR candy pieces, marshmallows and milk in small saucepan. Cook over low heat, stirring constantly, until bars are melted and mixture is smooth. (DO NOT CRUSH PEANUTS.) Pour into serving dish; let stand several minutes before serving. Serve warm over ice cream.

CHOCOLATE CARAMEL SAUCE

Yield: about ½ cup sauce

¼ cup HERSHEY'S Chocolate Flavored Syrup
1½ tablespoons milk
1 tablespoon butter
10 light caramels, unwrapped

Place HERSHEY'S Chocolate Flavored Syrup, milk, butter and caramels in small micro-proof bowl. Microwave on high (full power) for 1 to 2 minutes or until caramels are softened and mixture is melted and smooth when stirred. Serve warm over ice cream.

LIGHTER CHOCOLATE DESSERTS

DIET CHOCOLATE CHEESECAKES*

Yield: 6 servings

1½ teaspoons unflavored gelatine
2 tablespoons skim milk
⅓ cup skim milk
1 egg yolk
1½ tablespoons HERSHEY'S Cocoa
2 tablespoons sugar
¾ teaspoon vanilla
¾ cup low fat cottage cheese
1 egg white
1 tablespoon sugar
3 tablespoons graham cracker crumbs
Dash cinnamon
Fresh peach slices *or* naturally sweetened canned peach slices, drained

102 calories per serving

Sprinkle gelatine onto 2 tablespoons skim milk in blender container; let stand several minutes to soften. Meanwhile, heat ⅓ cup skim milk to boiling; pour into blender container and process until gelatine dissolves. Add egg yolk, HERSHEY'S Cocoa, 2 tablespoons sugar and the vanilla; process at medium speed until well blended. Add cottage cheese; blend at high speed until smooth. Pour into bowl; chill until mixture mounds from a spoon. Beat egg white until frothy; gradually add 1 tablespoon sugar and beat until stiff peaks form. Fold into chocolate mixture. Combine graham cracker crumbs and cinnamon; divide evenly among 6 paper-lined muffin cups (2½ inches in diameter). Divide chocolate evenly among prepared cups. Cover; chill several hours or overnight. Serve garnished with peach slices.

SKIM MILK HOT COCOA

Yield: two 7-ounce servings

2 tablespoons HERSHEY'S Cocoa
3 tablespoons sugar
¼ cup hot water
1½ cups skim milk
⅛ teaspoon vanilla

157 calories per serving

Blend HERSHEY'S Cocoa and sugar in small saucepan; gradually add hot water. Cook over medium heat, stirring constantly, until mixture boils; boil and stir for 2 minutes. Add milk; heat thoroughly. Stir occasionally; do not boil. Remove from heat; add vanilla. Serve hot.

COCOA GELATINE DESSERT

Yield: 3 servings

140 calories per serving

- 2 teaspoons unflavored gelatine
- ¼ cup cold water
- ⅓ cup nonfat dry milk powder
- 1 cup water
- 1 egg yolk, slightly beaten
- 1½ tablespoons HERSHEY'S Cocoa
- ⅛ teaspoon salt
- 3 tablespoons sugar
- 1 teaspoon vanilla
  Fresh *or* naturally sweetened canned fruit, drained

Sprinkle gelatine onto ¼ cup cold water; set aside. Combine milk powder and 1 cup water in small saucepan; blend in egg yolk, HERSHEY'S Cocoa and salt. Cook over medium heat, stirring constantly, until mixture just begins to boil; remove from heat. Stir in gelatine mixture, sugar and vanilla. Pour into individual dessert molds. Place plastic wrap gently on surface; chill until firm. Unmold desserts; serve garnished with fruit.

COCOA-DATE PORCUPINES

Yield: about 1½ dozen

with sugar substitute 47 calories per serving
with sugar 52 calories per serving

- 1 egg, slightly beaten
- 2 tablespoons sugar *or* sugar substitute to equal 2 tablespoons sugar
- 2 tablespoons HERSHEY'S Cocoa
- ½ cup finely chopped pitted dates
- 1 cup toasted rice cereal
- ¼ cup finely chopped nuts
- ½ cup flaked coconut

Combine egg, sugar or sugar substitute and HERSHEY'S Cocoa in small saucepan; add dates. Cook over medium heat, stirring constantly, until mixture almost boils. Cool 5 minutes; stir in cereal and nuts. Cool completely. Drop by teaspoonfuls into coconut; roll in coconut, forming into balls.

CHOCOLATE FILLED PEACHES

Yield: 6 servings

97 calories per serving

- ½ cup soft-style cream cheese
- 2 tablespoons HERSHEY'S Chocolate Flavored Syrup
- 1 packet aspartame-type low calorie sweetener
- 6 peach halves (16-ounce can) in extra light syrup, well-drained

Combine cream cheese, HERSHEY'S Chocolate Flavored Syrup and sweetener in small mixer bowl. Beat on medium speed until blended and smooth. Cover and chill until stiff enough to pipe through pastry bag, about 1 to 2 hours. Place each peach half, cut side up, in a dessert dish; chill. Place filling in pastry bag with open star tip; pipe into center of each peach. Serve immediately or chill.

Cocoa Gelatine Dessert, this page.